HOW TO START AND RUN

A SUCCESSFUL

HOME TYPING BUSINESS

Also by Peggy Glenn:

WORD PROCESSING PROFITS AT HOME

and

KEROSENE HEATERS: A Consumer's Review
DON'T GET BURNED! A Family Fire-Safety Guide
      (written with her husband, Gary A. Glenn)

How To Start and Run
A Successful
HOME TYPING
BUSINESS

by Peggy Glenn

Aames-Allen
PUBLISHING CO.

HOW TO START AND RUN A SUCCESSFUL HOME TYPING BUSINESS

by Peggy Glenn
foreword by Alma Vanasse, M.A.

AAMES-ALLEN PUBLISHING
1106 MAIN STREET
HUNTINGTON BEACH CA 92648-2719 USA
714/536-4926

Revised third edition. (Updated 4/84.)
Printed in the United States of America.
Delta Lithograph, Inc., Van Nuys, California.

Acknowledgement is made to the following for reprinted materials: p. 152, Dennis the Menace cartoon by permission of Hank Ketcham and © by Field Enterprises, Inc.,[T.M®]

Library of Congress Cataloging in Publication (CIP) Data
Glenn, Peggy.
How to start and run a successful home typing business.

Bibliography: p.
Includes index.
1. Home-based businesses--Handbooks, manual, etc. 2. Typewriting--Handbooks, manuals, etc. 3. Self-employed--Handbooks, manuals, etc. I. Title.
HD62.7.G55   1983   652.3'0068   83-3879
ISBN 0-936930-87-X
ISBN 0-936930-82-9 (pbk.)
ISBN 0-936930-83-7 (pbk./spiral)

- -

5 - 4 - 3 - 2 / 1

CONTENTS

to all who have put forth super-human
effort to help me finish this book...

and all who will read it and consider
my human-ness if a "typo" is found...

and to Gary, my love.

FOREWORD

The benefits to individuals who choose to work out of their homes are many—if the original plans for the business are well thought out. Peggy Glenn has written this very useful guide to help a beginner. The book has been written in a very professional way and includes many necessary details.

Peggy Glenn understands the needs of individuals (especially homemakers) and she has explored the most efficient way for them to launch their own careers. Novices will feel confident that they are following a tried and true method when they use her book to help set up their own home typing business (or as a guide for a different home-based business).

In addition to helping individuals set up their own home businesses, Peggy Glenn is willing to help people establish their own network system to support each other. This is a very powerful aid to this special group.

There are many creative individuals in their homes who have great ideas but lack the impetus to begin their venture. This book of Peggy Glenn's will fill the void that has existed because it has almost every answer to the questions: Where? Why? and How do I begin?

Alma Vanasse, M.A.
Career Guidance Specialist

Director, Women's Center
Saddleback College
Mission Viejo, California

ACKNOWLEDGEMENT

I'm indebted to a great many people for the faith they've shown in me and the patience and help they've given me in putting together this book.

Without the loyalty, encouragement, and assistance of my family, professional colleagues, and close friends, you wouldn't be reading this. **I** know who they are, **they** know who they are, and you **wouldn't** know who they are, so I won't mention all their names. For satisfaction of my own need to say "thanks", however, I must mention: my husband, Gary, whose love and support were always there; and Shasta Glenn, Jane Allison, Joe Flinn, Barbara Seese, Bernie Petitjean, Pat Blakeley, Barbara Erickson, Mindy Gaunt, Joan Woolard, and Ann Powell, Nancy Martin, Gene Hinze.

I owe a great deal to my parents and grandparents who instilled in me a long time ago a respect for words, whether I read them or wrote them, and a love of education. They gave me the time and opportunity to express myself, even when they disagreed with me. I was never without books or a library, and I'm grateful to be able to contribute to someone else's library now.

I also acknowledge you, the reader, and all who have read earlier editions. We do feel our worth, we will be successful, and we will elevate the image of the professional person who types (or word processes) at home.

INTRODUCTION

WHAT'S THIS BOOK ALL ABOUT, WHO IS IT FOR

This book is intended for your use in setting up a successful home-based typing business and running it for as long as it makes you happy. The information in this book can be applied whether you intend to have a small part-time business, or whether you plan on having a full-time business. (What you might find after awhile is that even a full-time business doesn't need to be 40 hours a week.)

While most of the information in this book is geared toward working in your home, most of the basics will be appropriate even if you choose to rent a small office away from your home.

I assume that you can type. As a general rule, if you can type a single page of double-spaced pica typing in 10 minutes with only 3 or 4 errors, you can make money at it. Those are the absolute minimum qualifications. If your skills aren't that sharp, take a short refresher course through your adult education deparment or at a community college.

If what you lack is current knowledge of office procedures -- maybe you've been away from the job world for a number of years -- try easing back into the profession by accepting temporary work through an agency. This approach doesn't involve the demoralizing ritual of looking, interviewing for, and having to leave permanent employment. With the temporary agency as the intermediary, either you or the employer is free to terminate the work relationship with no unpleasant confrontation.

The most rewarding and fulfilling aspect of a home-based typing business is that you are free to work whenever it is convenient for YOU: morning, afternoon, evenings, weekends, or any combination. Irregular work schedules -- yours or a family member's -- are more easily managed. You are also free to pursue your own personal activities.

The income is pleasant, too. Whether you earn money for extras, to help out with inflation's invasion of your lifestyle, or as your only source of revenue, you can see a direct correlation between how hard you work and how much money you bring in. You work to support you -- not some large company or obscure governmental agency.

In most all areas of the country, there is plenty of work to go around. Don't be afraid of competition. Instead develop a sense of cooperation. Network with other typists in your area referring customers within the network instead of losing them to inferior typists. Our public image climbs rapidly this way.

A natural spirit of competitive cooperation within a local group of typists will be beneficial to all. The work will retain a high quality. Yes, of course, you feel you're the best -- you should feel that way. That high degree of self-confidence will be reflected in all your contacts with customers and may be just the "extra" that will land you a job or contract. But retain some humility with that confidence. Realize that you can't possibly do all the work there is; someone else has to do some of it.

If there are three or four of you working in a particular area, get to know one another. Once you know each other, you may find that there are subtle differences in your skills and in the work you each like to do. These differences will help you determine just which typist is perfect for which customer when you need a referral. Conversely, if another typist wants to refer a customer to you, if she or he knows your particular strengths, both you and the customer will be happy.

In my area there were over two dozen typists to whom I referred customers. These typists returned the favor as well. The customer knew that he or she could expect the same professional work from all of us. That gave us good public relations and kept customers coming back over and over.

For instance, my strong area was academic typing, and I was especially strong in a few subject areas. If I received a request to type a psychology, nursing, or education paper, for example, I took it on gladly. However, if I got a math, chemistry, or computer science paper, I referred it to one of my colleagues.

As another example, most of my work experience had been at colleges and universities and most of Charlotte's experience (one of those colleagues I just mentioned) had been in the business world of property investment companies, real estate firms, accountants, and financial firms. We both advertised our typing businesses; and sometimes customers didn't look beyond our names to see what kind of work we specialized in. So we traded customers and everyone was happier.

WHAT'S THIS BUSINESS ALL ABOUT?

Do you believe myths? The two most common myths about small businesses -- and particularly home-based small businesses -- are:

1. It's complicated.

    Not so, it requires some time, some thought, some planning, some intuition, but it's not complicated.

2. It's only for the very brilliant or very rich.

    Not so again. Some of the richest people don't have the slightest idea about what makes a good idea work, nor do they have the "street" skills to make it work. And some of the most intelligent people don't have enough inner drive or common sense to follow through on a plan.

Cottage industries -- another term for home-based businesses -- have experienced unprecedented growth over the last 10 years, and especially during the last 3-4 years. Where once there were small, very part-time businesses that folks worked at in their spare time, there are now full-time businesses that folks use to support themselves.

Women represent a substantial percentage of these home-based businesses. A recent United States Chamber of Commerce report states that, "Fifteen million businesses in the United States file IRS reports under Schedule C (sole proprietor). Only 5 million of those businesses (that's less than one-third, friends) list an address away from home. The other 10 million list home addresses. Many of those businesses are operated by women."

I see home-based typists or freelance secretaries as the way of the future in a lot of areas. I firmly believe that the demand will increase for skilled typists who can produce written documents of superior quality at reasonable rates. Just as word processors are helping to cut costs in business and industry, many major companies now pay well to have work done outside the firm -- anything to avoid adding another permanent person to the payroll. That's okay.

Some companies try to solve their problems by hiring temporary employees when there's a work crunch or when a permanent employee is out for an extended period of time. However, a company pays on the average of $4 an hour more for a temporary employee than they pay the regular employee. Yet the temporary employee is probably paid at or slightly below the regular employee's scale. You know the temporary agency is getting a share of that extra.

So why not cut out the middleman? Become a sort of temporary employee to businesses, lawyers, doctors and medical labs, people who are going to college and need papers typed, and writers who hate to face the typewriter to make the final copy of a manuscript. Be an independent contractor, your own boss. Work at their place or at your home.

You can afford to undercut your competition a little bit in the beginning to gain a stable source of customers. But don't be a bargain! Bargain rates attract only bargain customers with bargain-quality work that is often boring and unpleasant.

Be a **PROFESSIONAL!** Think of yourself as a **PRO-FESSIONAL!** Conduct yourself as a **PROFESSIONAL!** Before long you'll be **paid** as a professional, **treated** as one, and be able to get Lloyds of London to insure your hands and fingers (or whatever you type with).

The first step in the process is to look closely at: your reasons for starting your own business, your personality, your budget, and your family situation and any special circumstances. Don't be shy, and don't be superficial. Take a good hard look as Chapter 1 tells you how.

*   *   *   *

P.S. I assume that the majority of people who will read this book are women. If you are a man, please don't take offense, and please know that I am well aware that many men are excellent typists and well-qualified to run home-based businesses. Practicality, though, dictates that this book be directed to the female audience just as a book on fixing motorcycles will probably be directed at males. Consider my dilemma at making this whole thing non-sexist, and if you are a man, please bear up under the same pressure women have faced in the press for centuries.

P.S. #2 Before we go any further, I'd also like to mention that this book has been typed -- over the objec-tions of most everyone in the publishing industry who says a book should be typeset -- for you. But I know you, you're like me, and we're used to reading type-written material in just this large format. BUT, looks can be deceiving, too. This book was "typed" on my Dictaphone Dual-Display (Model 3000) word processor without whose help countless hours of editing and revis-ing would have been impossible. It was "typed" using a metal print wheel that looks just like the Courier 10 typewriter element. Fooled you, but only because I care about you. Happy reading.

Thanks, PG

UNCERTAINTY

Uncertainty and expectation are the joys of life. Security is an insipid thing, and the overtaking and possessing of a wish discovers the folly of the chase.

— WILLIAM CONGREVE, 1695

2
CLOSE LOOK

Whenever you start anything new, you should look closely and carefully at all the sides, all the angles, all the springboards and the roadblocks or temporary detours. What can and will support you emotionally and financially? I hope you take each of these next sections seriously. If I've left out a question that applies to your life, YOU ask it. When you have satisfactory answers to all the questions, take the next step.

It's difficult to estimate how many times people have asked me, "Why on earth did you ever give up all the security and benefits of working for a big university medical school to go into your own business?"

WHY?

I usually answer, that after 7 years in the same department I had received only one promotion, a few meager salary raises, but always more responsibility "because we know you're so capable." They offered me the position of Administrative Assistant, but I didn't feel it was worth it without combat pay!

I figured if I was as capable and smart as my superiors kept telling me I was, I ought to be smart enough to get out of there and capitalize on <u>what</u> I knew and could do, and <u>how</u> <u>well</u> I could do it.

A former head of career development at UCLA's Placement and Career Planning Center once told a reporter, "There are rare cases where a secretary ends up being a vice president, but most secretaries stay secretaries." I think that what I saw in the academic world is true everywhere -- in business, in law, in government, in medicine, in industry. Secretaries are valued, but exploited. Many, like you and me, are leaving. The shortage of qualified secretaries becomes more critical each year.

Now, in my own business I have all the promotional opportunity I'll ever need. In any given day I can be:

"Go-fer"
President
Secretary
Treasurer
Receptionist
Bill Collector
Purchasing Agent
Custodial Service
Appointments Clerk
Advertising Director, etc., etc., etc.

Another thing that bothered me when I was working was watching the older secretaries -- some of whom had been at the same job for many years -- taking medical leaves and medical retirements in ever-increasing numbers. They were having heart attacks, open-heart surgery, problems with high blood pressure, ulcers, etc. I was only 32 and didn't like the prospect.

A recent study by the National Heart, Lung, and Blood Institute found that the risk of heart disease is twice as prevalent among working women who work in clerical positions than in any other group of women, working outside the home or not. The most vulnerable were those clerical workers who had children at home. Too much to do in too little time with too much stress?

The study found that secretaries and other clerical workers had the highest degree of suppressed anger. The women in the study also complained about unsupportive bosses, that they had almost no control over their jobs, had no freedom of movement (needing permission to leave their desk or use the rest room), and generally felt frustrated and powerless with no one to talk to about their problems. Those same feelings -- frustration, lack of control, no appreciation -- were part of my motivation.

That study was reported in the February 1980 Journal of Public Health. You might want to find a copy in your library and read through the article.

Another big issue for me was family time. In order to take time off for sick kids, for example, I had to lie to my employer. Tending to kids' illnesses wasn't a valid use of my sick time, so it was lie or take the time without pay. In either case it was the old guilt heaped on with a ladle. Yes, I felt a responsibility to my job. Of course I did. But I felt a much greater responsibility to my kids. After awhile, I tired of arguing about it. I felt I needed more and more "mental health" days off. Was it burnout?

The last issue for me, and probably one that will fit the majority of working clerical women, was money. I really felt underpaid -- grossly exploited if you want the truth. Beyond that, by the time I deducted taxes and direct work expenses, it looked as if I was working for about $2 an hour. When I came to that "bottom line" it was "quittin' time." I was convinced I could make more money for less work and with less aggravation. I was right.

You can probably see that these feelings created a seething anger. You may be feeling that anger yourself. Please take my advice and deal with and resolve that anger before you plunge head-long into your business. If you don't, the first unpleasant or distressing encounter with a difficult customer will cause all those feelings to rush back, and you'll find yourself comparing the customer to the old boss or the old bureaucracy. This may be an unfair comparison. Allow the past situation to be forgotten, recognize that your new business will have trying times, and maybe even say out loud to yourself, "Maybe that guy was a drip, but this still beats working for someone else, because if he calls again, I won't have to work for him."

What personality or wishes have you identified in yourself? Are you ambitious, willing to take a risk, feeling trapped in a corporate world, eager to take your idea and run with it? Go ahead and run. No one holds a stop-watch but you, but there are hundreds of fans on the sidelines watching you stride by and wishing they had the guts to run with you.

WHY NOT?

Another of my favorite answers to that question, "Why?" is usually another question: "Why not?" I know that's not a fair answer, but I mean it? Why shouldn't I have taken a chance?

Several years ago I adopted a personal philosophy of having no "why-nots" or "what-ifs" in my life. I never wanted to look back and ask myself those questions or have regrets.

Some call it Yankee stubbornness, others call it the emotion of the '70s (me-first). I prefer to think of myself as an incurable individualist. I want to do it my way, do what I like best, do it for the people I choose, and with as much harmony with my personal life as possible.

If I take on work and it turns out that I don't like it or the customer, I don't accept it again. If a customer is unpleasant, I'm simply too busy the next time he or she calls. I refuse graciously because I can't afford bad publicity, but I end up controlling my professional life. More about that process in Chapter 9, "Customers."

Another big advantage for me was the freedom of choice in my wardrobe and working conditions. I prefer to wear sweat pants and t-shirts while sitting for hours at a typewriter or word-processor keyboard. Occasionally if I wake up early, I'll even work a few hours in my robe and slippers. Now, tell me an office where that would be appropriate? No, that's not the kind of attire that would readily be accepted out in the professional world of pantyhose, matched outfits, and color-coordinated accessories. But those early morning hours can be productive, and I had no dress code in my business.

No dress code, that is, unless I was seeing customers. But, and this is an absolute, I never allowed a customer to see me in sweat pants or in my robe and slippers. Granted, they were interested in the professional appearance of their work more than the wardrobe of their typist, but there was more involved here than just the simple typing transaction. All their business dealings with me would depend on their perception of the extent of my professionalism. If I needed to firmly discuss a bill they thought was too high, I needed to have been "seen" as a professional business-woman from the start. How do you successfully argue over a $250 discrepancy when dressed in faded jeans and an oversize flannel shirt with the sleeves rolled up, or in shorts and a halter?

Occasionally a "veteran" customer would catch me in my apron while I was fixing dinner or cleaning up after it. I didn't worry about it too much then. I always did good work! And they appreciated that I was available evening hours. Sometimes I'd invite a special or long-standing customer to have a cup of coffee with us . . . no different than if my office were in the center of town or in a high-rise office building.

A light touch of flu, a cold, or an attack of the springtime sneezies no longer meant I'd have to take a day off from work, either. I may not have put in a full day, but there was no rule in my business that said I couldn't type for an hour or so, take a nap, and type some more.

When I had my "real job" I had to call in sick during those times . . . and you all know about calling in and telling the boss you're sick for the day. The news is not exactly greeted with enthusiasm. Ah-h-h, those guilt trips are just a memory now.

Examine your own life for "what-ifs" and "why-nots" and make the best choice for you.

PERSONALITY PLUS

According to research conducted by the Small Business Administration and women's advocacy groups, there are certain personality traits in a woman that are necessary to insure that a self-employment venture will be profitable and successful.

Organization, dependability, self-motivation, confidence, perseverance, flexibility, authority, firmness, and tolerance are some of the key personality elements to look for in deciding if this kind of business is for you.

Organization and dependability are what will impress your customers and allow you to meet deadlines with a minimum of personal struggle. Self-motivation, confidence, and perseverance are what will keep you going when the business is slow and you have to rustle up more work.

Flexibility is an absolute must if you are to mesh your business and personal lives successfully. Authority, firmness, and an amazing amount of tolerance are essential in dealing with unpleasant customers under difficult circumstances.

If you are shy, easily-intimidated, self-doubting, or insecure, you will find it more difficult. This doesn't mean you can't try, and it doesn't automatically spell failure, but it definitely means you will have to work very hard. Perhaps simply recognizing these traits will help you overcome them or compensate for them.

Take a close look at your personality strengths and weaknesses. If you have a majority of positive traits and a minority of negative ones, it is probably a worthwhile gamble. Try it and see.

I do feel obligated to briefly discuss some very real "Why not's." I have talked with or heard from many women who tried their very best but were destined for failure before they started simply because their very best wasn't anywhere near good enough.

FIRST, be honest with yourself about your skills. If you repeatedly turn out work that looks messy, contains errors, or wasn't done on time or according to the directions, you will fail. Repeat customers is the backbone of this business; strong word-of-mouth referrals from old customers to new ones are the legs that support that backbone.

SECOND, be honest about your personality. If you're uncomfortable about meeting strangers, if you tremble at the thought of having customers come to your home, if you can't look a customer in the eye and tell him or her how much you charge, if you feel guilty when it's time to raise your prices, if you can't take a compliment, a home-based typing business is going to be a real struggle. The only way I see you overcoming this is to either deal by mail with writers or to hire a "front person" who will make all business contacts for you and a messenger who will pick up and deliver all work from clients.

THIRD, be honest about your family situation. You must have the support -- at least a little bit -- of the people who live in the same house with you, and even those close relatives who have a habit of telling you what, when, where, and how to run your life. If you live alone, be prepared for the difference between the camaraderie of working in an office and the solitude of working at home. Accept the work-day loneliness if you like it (some people work best that way, I do), or develop extra social contacts if you'll miss that aspect of your work the most.

UPDATE

Many things change with time. Most notably for you is the fact that IPTN, the Independent Professional Typists Network, referred to in my books and in magazine or newspaper stories, has been disbanded. IPTN was a very good idea, but there weren't enough people who were self-employed at home who were able to commit the time and energy that was necessary to sustain a professional organization.

There are a few local groups that still flourish in some areas of the country although I am not aware of their meeting places or schedules. You can check with someone who is in business, or watch the calender notices in the business section of your local newspaper.

PASS, the Professional Association of Secretarial Services, has also disbanded for essentially the same reason as stated above.

At this writing, I do know of several national groups that would be appropriate for you to consider. Your local library's reference librarian can help you find current addresses for the national headquarters of such organizations as: National Association of Women Business Owners (NAWBO), National Alliance of Homebased Businesswomen (NAHB), National Association of Secretarial Services (NASS).

In addition, watch the notices in your local newspaper for meetings of other networking-type groups of business owners such as the Leads Club, local business groups, and perhaps your Chamber of Commerce.

I'd like to recommend a few books which deal with the philosophy of working in the non-traditional way, and which also address the personality aspects of making self-employment successful.

THE ENTREPRENEURIAL WOMAN, by Sandra Winston.
    Published by Newsweek Books and Bantam

THE BEST OF BOTH WORLDS, by Joan Wester Anderson.
    Published by Betterway Publications, Inc.

THE NEW ENTREPRENEURS, by Terri & Nona Dawe Tepper
    Published by Universe Books

MINDING MY OWN BUSINESS, by Marjorie McVicar and
    Julia Craig. Published by Richard Marek
    Publishers, Inc.

EARNING MONEY WITHOUT A JOB and
555 WAYS TO EARN EXTRA MONEY, by Jay Conrad
    Levinson. Published by Holt, Rinehart and
    Winston

BUDGET MATTERS

If you intend to use the home-based typing business for supplemental money or as a part-time job rather than as your sole support, the financial issues are not as critical for you. But read on anyway; much of this next part will be helpful to you.

If you are leaving a "real job" and setting up this business as your sole source of support, examine your budget carefully. Look for ways to save, carefully plan to be able to pay all your bills.

FIRST, ask yourself these questions.

1. How much actual cash do I need to make it from week to week, month to month? (Rent, food, utilities, charge accounts, car payment, etc.)

2. How much money is my "real job" costing me and can I save on any or all of those expenses? (Clothes, transportation, child care, fast foods, taxes, dues or fees, etc.)

3. Do I have anything in the bank or credit union to get me over a rough spot, through a slow month, or to take care of unexpected bills?

4. Do I have to go into debt to set up, or can I do it on a pay-as-I-go basis? Do I have any credit in my own name? If I take a loan, will I be able to pay it back?

5. Is there anyone else depending on my income?

6. Can I be stingy with myself until the money starts coming in regularly? Can I set a budget and keep to it? Can I resist temptation and impulses and hang onto my money?

To plan your budget, take advantage of many excellent books in your local library and/or pamphlets put out by the federal government. These give excellent advice on figuring a household budget, setting up a small business, and keeping track of all of the money -- coming in and going out.

A couple of my favorites are:

HOW TO PROSPER IN YOUR OWN BUSINESS, by Brian R. Smith. Published by the Stephen Greene Press

HOW TO START, RUN, AND STAY IN BUSINESS, by Greg and Patty Kishel. Published by John Wiley and Sons

Refigure your income/outgo budget every six months. Your priorities may shift and you may find that one area needs adjusting to fit your new lifestyle.

14

My budgeting strategy was rather simple. I used my husband's paycheck to pay all the bills and we used my earnings to eat. With 3 teenagers to feed, that was motivation enough, believe me. The first steak was cause for celebration, and the first dinner in a restaurant was something like a Hollywood happening for us.

SECOND, small business experts advise that you set weekly income goals that are at least 25% higher than what you figured you MUST have. The income will fluctuate for a while, so in any week where you earn more than your goal, put the extra money aside to help you with a week that is under-goal.

THIRD, mark 10% of your total earnings as sacred and absolutely untouchable. Deposit the money in some sort of interest-bearing account. That first 10% deduction should be used for paying insurance premiums, for taking your "benefits" (sick days, vacations, etc.), and as a small hedge against double-digit inflation.

Earmark a second 10% for re-investing in your business. Use this money to pay for equipment maintenance contracts, to buy supplies, for additional advertising, and for generally improving your business.

Now set aside an additional 5% for fun -- pure and simple fun! It's vital to your mental health. Without some fun, this business becomes as much of a drudge as your old job and can lead to health problems as well. When that happens, you've defeated one of the primary reasons for being self-employed.

According to a fact sheet recently released by the Women's Bureau of the U. S. Department of Labor, "it is frequently the woman's earnings which raise a family out of poverty." They also report that, "a majority of women work because of economic need." In 1978 almost two-thirds of the women in the labor force were single, widowed, divorced or separated, or if married, their husbands were earning less than $10,000 a year. The 1980 census figures are even higher.

With those facts and figures in mind, be sure you analyze your budget carefully so you can set your income goals correctly.

FOURTH, now that you've figured out how much money you'll need, what resources do you have to get started? Do you have any available cash? any savings? any assets to trade for what you need? a good credit rating so you can buy equipment or arrange a lease? This will be discussed more thoroughly in Chapter 4, but start thinking about it now. Start listing all your financial pluses and minuses so that when you start planning your actual purchases, you'll know where you stand.

FAMILY MATTERS

How supportive will your family be? Will they intrude when you have a deadline? Will they complain that the typewriter noise is interfering with their TV enjoyment? Will they understand when you send out for hamburgers three nights in a row while working on a deadline?

Will they help with housekeeping duties at all? Will they take phone messages when you're out? If you have small children, will you be able to afford a sitter, or will you have to wait to type until they are in bed?

These will be the hardest questions to answer, because you aren't the one who can answer them. Your family might not be able to answer them, either, because they don't know what to expect and can only speculate as to how they will act and feel. In addition, they may be less than honest about their commitment to your new venture because they don't want to hurt your feelings.

I'll be perfectly honest with you. This is the part of the business I found the hardest. My husband still has a little difficulty being known as "Peggy Glenn's husband." He's also not very happy when I work at night.

My kids resented it sometimes, too, especially when a deadline interfered with their plans for my involvement in their social life. (It was a different story, though, when they wanted me to type a school paper for them at 9:30 at night so they could take it to school at 7:30 the next morning.)

I actually got more help with housework when I had my "real job." It was easier for my family to identify that I was "working" when I was out of the house. The way in which I solved my dilemma, at least temporarily, was to go on a strike. After I made my point, we had a calm discussion at which I pulled my best dictator act and announced that they had two choices:

(1)   they could all help with chores on a propor-
       tional share basis (hubby included); or
(2)   they could all chip in equal shares and we'd
       hire a housekeeper.

The vote was for option #2. As teenagers, the kids all had the ability to make a little money. This plan worked out rather well. They were embarrassed to let things get too out of control, because they didn't want the housekeeper to see how careless they were. It was okay for Mom to scrub toothpaste out of the bath- room sink, but it was out of the question to have the housekeeper see how poor their aim was.

This arrangement was quite successful until the housekeeper moved to Kansas. We never hired another one, our oldest daughter moved into her own apartment, and I just resigned myself to having a "comfortable" house instead of a clean one.

When I first started talking about quitting my job and trying self-employment, my husband was very uneasy. He's one of the quiet cautious types, and he wasn't sure I could bring in enough money. At the time, we really depended on my income. We still depend on my income. I proved myself, but his hesitancy was difficult to accept when I was feeling so enthusiastic.

He was skeptical, and I think his skepticism just made me work all the harder to prove I could do it. I told him that I was certain I had a saleable service, especially since we live in an area with lots of colleges and universities. I was confident that I could generate more than enough steady business with some well-placed advertising.

SPECIAL CIRCUMSTANCES

"Hotel, motel," visitors, recreation activities

If you live in a popular vacation area of the country (Southern California, Hawaii, Florida, etc.), will out-of-town visiting friends and relatives pose a problem for you? How will they react when you beg out of a day's activity to finish a term paper, a financial report, a legal brief, a doctor's dictation, or a writer's manuscript? (Very often, even well-meaning neighbors will forget that you're really in business.)

Handling your hostess duties and your business duties will often require all the tact and diplomacy you can muster. If you always treat your home-based business seriously, I don't think you'll encounter too many problems. No doubt, you'll have the opportunity to balance business and hostess duties more easily than if you had an 8 to 5'er, but don't lose sight of your commitment to your customers and their deadlines.

Physical disabilities

If you're physically disabled, do you need anyone to help you run your business? If you're a paraplegic, you might want to hire someone to help with pickup and delivery to inaccessible buildings if your specialty is commercial typing. If you're a quadriplegic, you'll probably need an assistant to feed the paper into the typewriter and remove it when you're done.

If you have any speech impairment -- cerebral palsy for instance -- you'll want to consider arranging for a person to help with telephone messages. If you're deaf, you'll also need a message service or a TTY.

None of these disabilities should be seen as road-blocks, however. With the advice in this book and sound guidance from a vocational counselor, there is no reason a physically disabled person can't make good money with a typing business. An occupational thera-pist reminded me that quadriplegics have reached amaz-ing speeds with a mouth stick or a forehead appliance. Determination and skill usually win out over adversity.

Family "roadblocks"

If you live with your parents, will they permit phone calls and visits from customers at irregular hours? If they need extra convincing that you're not off on another hare-brained idea, try enlisting their help. This may get them off your back and on your team. Can you put in your own phone line? Will younger or older brothers or sisters interfere with your work?

Will the family be courteous to customers on the phone and at the door? Will they take messages when you are out? Can you say no to friends who want to socialize when you have a deadline to meet?

Childcare

If you have young children, I strongly recommend that you make arrangements for a sitter or child care. Even if you don't work while your youngster(s) visits the sitter or child care center, you'll enjoy the free time, if only for an hour every other day or so.

I have talked with scores of mothers of young chil-dren. One woman has a legal transcription service at home, several have medical or general typing businesses at home, many type for students, another sells Tupper-ware, and they all agree that a reliable babysitter or child care center is an absolute necessity.

I can't talk from experience because my children were teenagers when I started my business. But all the women who have young children gave me the same answer -- it was unanimous -- hire a babysitter or use child care on a regular basis. The single mothers were

more emphatic than the married ones. They all said
they needed an occasional break from mothering duties.

Try also to remember that your children are a part
of you, they're a part of your home, but they aren't a
big part of your business. Define their role early,
and redefine as they grow up and their needs change.

> Is the goal so far away?
> Far, how far no tongue can say?
> Let us dream our dream today.
> -- Alfred Tennyson

SUMMARY

So now you have looked at the whys and why-nots,
you've looked at your personality, your financial situation, your family status and any special circumstances.
Take a week or so to mull it all over in your mind;
talk with your family, friends or relatives, or anyone
who can give you support and be a good sounding board.
Make a two-column list of your own "why" reasons and
"why not" reasons. Make another list of your strengths
and weaknesses. Make one more list of your overall
goals -- for this month, for 6 months from now, for one
year from now.

Recognize that you have limitations and admit to
them. Try to point them out to your family, too. Now
that you are working at home, it's true that you will
have a little more time for household responsibilities.
You can type at the same time that the dishwasher or
washer and dryer are running; you can type while the
crockpot does its thing. But it's impossible to type
and vacuum, type and dust, or type and mop floors or
fix an elaborate smorgasbord luncheon.

Look at it your way and make a decision based on
your unique needs. I told you how I did it, but no
other person's life is like mine. Pick and choose what
works best for you.

If you're really scared, try the home typing business on a part-time basis while you still have your
"real job." If you haven't been working, you don't
have as much to lose, but self-employment can be just
as scary, if not more so, since you're re-entering the
work world and don't know if it's a jungle or paradise.
It won't be a bed of roses, not all the time. But once

the business gets off to a start and the profits trickle in, it'll be worth it.

Look at the comparison below. I've often marveled at how what is natural, ordinary, and accepted in a self-employment environment is completely foreign and forbidden in a traditional work environment. There again is that aspect of are you the one who is BEING controlled or are you the one IN control?

This is the "BEFORE" and the "AFTER" Peggy Glenn as seen through the eyes of former co-workers and present colleagues respectively.

BEFORE	AFTER
stubborn	determined, persistent
outspoken/critical	courage to stand up
conceited, brash	sure, confident
nosy	sharp, inquisitive
just a secretary	professional typist
$4.00/hour	$15.00/hour (minimum)

I like the new list better than the old, and I'm still the same person. But now my ways are acceptable and before they were cause for friction. What will your two lists look like? Will you be pleased? Ready to read on? Let's go! There's an ancient Chinese proverb that states, "A journey of a thousand miles starts with the first step." You don't have to go a thousand miles, you've already taken several giant steps, so how 'bout a few more?

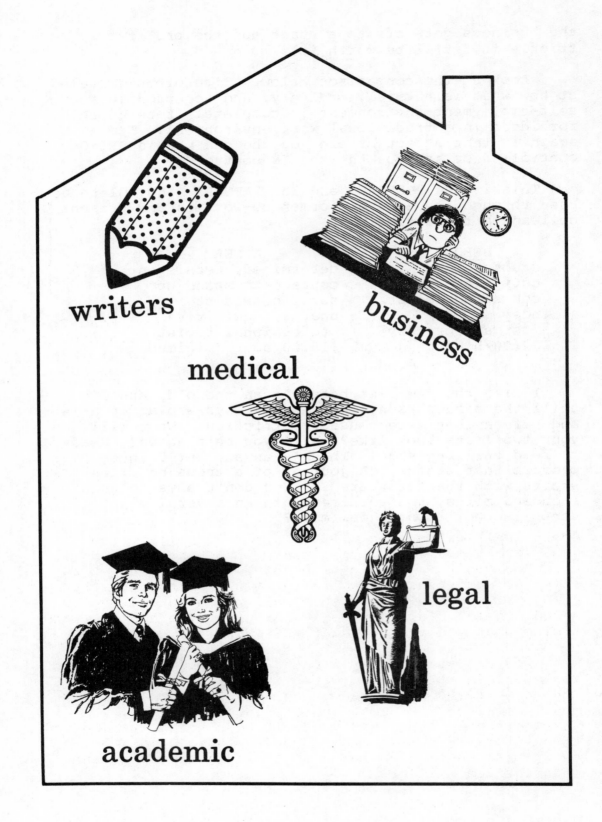

writers

business

medical

academic

legal

SKILLS/MARKETS

    This book is intended for the person who has average or better typing skills; but don't be frightened away if you are a beginner or if your skills are rusty. If you have some time to invest and are willing to learn, you, too, can be successful at a home-based typing business.

THE BEGINNER

    As a general rule, once you can type a single page of double-spaced, non-technical text with pica type and standard academic margins in 10 minutes (with no more than three errors), you are ready to hang out your shingle. This is the bare minimum. Although typing speed isn't extraordinarily critical for all typing jobs (sometimes you'll be given written or dictated work you can't read or understand), typing speed of at least 50 words-per-minute is the minimum industry standard. If you can't type that well, then be willing to spend a great deal of time learning to type and/or practicing what you learned many years ago.

    How are you going to learn? Probably the best way is to enroll in a typing class through your public school system's adult education department or at a community college. In most cases these classes will be free or nearly free, and you will be able to use modern typewriters. In some areas, you can enroll in job-retraining centers to learn or brush up on typing and other office skills.

    If you already know how to type but are extremely slow, then practice is what you need. Again, enrolling in an intermediate typing class may be your best bet. If you have a typewriter and can practice at home, do it. Type letters to friends, retype stories from magazines and newspapers, type, type, type! Many public libraries in large cities have coin-operated typewriters available. My librarian tells me that she knows of no full-service library in the country that doesn't have a typing instruction book, either. Perhaps your typing skills are in fine shape, but you're rusty about current practices, procedures, and formats in the business world. Working for a temporary agency will help you upgrade your skills and may also help familiarize you with the current office machines.

You might also consider an excellent book:

BRUSHING UP ON YOUR CLERICAL SKILLS, by Eve Steinberg. Arco Publishing

If you're reading up this book of mine, it's evidence that you are seriously considering typing or word processing at home. With just a little more determination, some time, faith in yourself, and acceptable typing skills, you can do it. You really can!

THE EXPERIENCED WORKER

So, now, if you are an acceptable or better typist, how can you match your skills with a particular market? Start by carefully looking (and listing again) your skill assets. Is there any subject area in which you have expertise: from prior employment, from volunteer work, from personal interests? Have you learned any special terminology from your spouse, children, friends, parents, or from a previous job?

Next, is there a need for your special skills where you live? Will there be a demand for you and your vocabulary or talents or special competencies? Be sure you match the available work with your available skills. A mis-match could be disaster. For instance, if your background is agriculture, mining, or forestry, you may not have much of a market in the middle of Chicago. By the same token, you may not do well with academic typing in an industrial area.

What extra do you have that will make you just one notch above the competition? Do you have excellent grammar and punctuation skills? (That alone will make you a lifesaver in a nation that is increasingly illiterate on paper.) Are you a competent editor and can you "fix up" reports, letters, proposals, and manuscripts?

Are you fluent in any language besides English? Can you take shorthand, and would you be willing to do it over the telephone? Do you have bookkeeping skills that you can combine with your typing skills to offer a more full-service program to your customers? Do you have additional "side" skills such as calligraphy, graphic arts ability, a notary's license or seal?

Using plain paper or a steno pad, make a list, such as the one below, of all your experience and side skills, whether you were paid for them or whether you acquired them by doing volunteer work.

— PAID —

- Store clerk - people skills handle money

- Secretary - trucking company
  bills of lading, customer contact, driver schedules, payroll, interstate commerce

- Admin. Ass't — school district personnel, contracts, proposals, government reports

— VOLUNTEER —

Scout leader - travel, meetings
Neighborhood Watch - speakers, programs, travel, newsletter, mailings

WHAT ARE THE MAJOR MARKET CATEGORIES

In my experience, there are basically five major markets for the home-based typist: academic, business or commercial, medical, legal, and professional writers. Within each of these areas, of course, are sub-specialties; and as I explore each of them, be thinking about your experience and where you can put it to use in the most pleasurable and profitable manner. Making money and having fun IS possible. Trust me.

ACADEMIC TYPING

This sort of typing covers everything from a 3-page book report for a high-school student to a textbook written by a university professor. In between are: term papers, essays, research reports, take-home exams, masters theses, doctoral dissertations, course outlines, grant proposals, resumes, and curriculum vitae.

In an academic typing business, you may not see all of these things, but you will certainly see a variety. The most valuable skills you can have in doing this form of work are attention to details and accurate spelling, punctuation, and grammar.

A strong editing ability will be an asset if you work for post-graduate students, for faculty members, or for adults who are returning to school to obtain an academic degree to supplement earlier vocational train-ing. Today, many people who received vocational degrees to enter their chosen field (nurses, police officers, teachers), now find that they need an aca-demic degree or an advanced academic degree to be pro-moted. (You know the new line, "I don't care how well you do your job, do you have a college degree?") If you have the ability to "translate" their occupational jargon into academically-acceptable language, you will never go hungry.

I feel that this is the most lucrative, most flex-ible, and most readily-available market for the home-based typist. A metropolitan or suburban area is very likely to contain a high percentage of people who attend classes at some level beyond high school.

Think for a minute of all of your neighbors, rela-tives, friends, and co-workers who are going to school. Then think of all the people who are in their classes.

26

Multiply that by the number of classes at their schools. There's your market!

If you live in an area that is close to a college or university, the possibilities are even better. Now your market extends to the faculty and staff employees of the institution as well. Many public colleges and universities are sadly understaffed clerically because of budget problems, so the faculty members are forced to go elsewhere to get any professional-advancement or personal work typed.

You may have some competition in this area from the secretaries at the schools. But remember, you can be available during the day when they're working. You can take care of the rush job while they're busy. If you are one of those secretaries, do as I did. Use your experience to its best advantage by leaving the confines of a "real job" and being available for the customer who needs your expertise.

One word of caution for the moonlighting college or university secretary: Be very careful that you don't use your employer's time or materials for your own business. First of all this is unethical. It may also be a violation of your employment contract and grounds for instant dismissal if a complaint is filed. In addition, it may be viewed as conflict of interest and result in a heavy fine and/or dismissal, especially if you work for a governmental agency. Check your employee handbook if you have any questions.

If you don't have academic experience, but feel that you can learn to do the work, there are a variety of style manuals you should become familiar with:

APA (AmPsycholAssoc)	-- Publication Manual
Campbell & Ballou	-- Form and Style: Theses, Reports, Term Papers
MLA (ModLangAssoc)	-- MLA Handbook for Writers of Research Papers, Theses, and Dissertations
Turabian	-- A Manual for Writers of Term Papers, Theses, and Dissertations

These paperback books can usually be found in any
college or university bookstore. They are also available in large commercial bookstores (B. Dalton, Walden-
books, etc.). Read through these manuals carefully and
thoroughly. Once you are familiar with the rules and
formats, you will save valuable time. After you work
with them a short while, the styles become second
nature.

Other professional groups have style manuals and
publication handbooks which deal with specialized
areas: geologists, anthropologists, biologists, physi-
cists, chemists, engineers, computer specialists, etc.
Ask your customer if there is any special manual or
format you are supposed to follow. If he or she has a
copy of the manual or instructions, ask to use the copy
while you type the paper, and then buy your own.

If you'll be working for students at one college
or university in particular, become familiar with any
special requirements of that institution. Very often
all post-graduate work (master and doctoral degrees)
must conform to the institution's own special format
rules. Become familiar with the person or committee at
the campus who is responsible for reviewing all these
papers, and obtain a copy of the manuscript preparation
guidelines for your own use and information.

BUSINESS OR COMMERCIAL TYPING

With a little ingenuity, this business and commercial typing can be done successfully at home also.
Many small businesses and professional offices are in
need of extra secretarial support. They may not have
the finances or the workload to justify a full-time
position, but nearly all of them need some form of
clerical help.

One very excellent business customer for the home-
based typist is another person who is also working from
home: consultants, sales people, small manufacturing
operations, etc. The "cottage industry" explosion gets
greater and greater each year that money gets tighter
and commercial office space becomes more expensive.
Conventions and professional meetings are another
source of business work.

The possibilities are limitless in this wide-open
business and commercial area. As just a few examples,
you can type:

1. menus for small restaurants and coffee shops

2. correspondence, mailing lists, and brochures for social groups, civic groups, associations, church groups, etc.

3. real estate listings or financing proposals for independent real estate salespeople or brokers

4. general office work for all small businesses

5. invoicing and collection duties for small shipping or manufacturing companies

6. any kind of correspondence at all for the general public (complaint letters, letters to explain misunderstandings, holiday letters, community or club newsletters)

7. job resumes and letters of introduction

8. consultants' reports or correspondence, ranging from a psychologist's report, or an environmental impact report (lovingly known as an EIR), to a management proposal, a financial report, or a feasibility study, and more.

Think of your experience. What have you done that would lend itself well to another small business and provide valuable clerical support to that small business? Have you worked for freight or trucking companies? Do you have a banking background? Do you know the plumbing business inside and out? Real estate? Insurance? Automobile sales and service?

I could fill up the rest of this book just asking you questions. But instead, I'll let you have the fun. Find out what you can offer the business world in your locale that no one else is offering. Or how you can do it better, more creatively.

*   *   *   *

I've heard of a few things just recently that show some ingenuity.

One woman provides a secretary/message service for traveling sales representatives. She has such clients as: a salesman for medical supplies, a salesman for printing press supplies and equipment, and a saleswoman for sportswear. She takes messages for them, types letters to their customers, maintains their mailing lists, and helps prepare their periodic sales and marketing reports.

One of her clients is also president of a professional organization, so she prepares that association's newsletter every other month and maintains all the files, correspondence, membership lists, etc., for that association.

Another woman works exclusively for small property-investment companies. She types agreements and proposals for only five companies, but that keeps her comfortably busy. She offers quick service, checks all the math, provides pick-up and delivery at $2 a trip, and is ACCURATE! She told me that she once discovered a $22,000 error in an early draft of a proposal, pointed it out to the investment company before the proposal was presented to anyone else, which saved the company considerable embarrassment, and she received a $50 bonus and a dozen roses! Now, I grant you, $50 might not sound like much for discovering a $22,000 error, but the proposal was only two pages long and her bill was only $17. I think a $50 bonus on a $17 bill is something to be proud of!

Another woman has some writing background and has also worked for an advertising agency. She prepares a newsletter and mailing labels for a small neighborhood grocery store. The store is fighting to compete in the world of the large conglomerate chain markets, and the owner pays her well to help him put "polish" on his newsletter.

She says that the store owner is convinced that he can attribute his increased sales to her help with the newsletter. He says that his customers appreciate the personalized touch. She is part of that and feels good about it. That's one of those extras -- pride -- that is so often missing in a standard secretarial job.

*   *   *   *

With just these three very different examples, you can see how varied the possibilities are for you. The work is there, you just have to go after it and make every customer glad that you walked into his or her store, office, company, or group.

30

If you need any help brushing up on your skills at letter writing, preparing reports, setting up resumes, and any business correspondence, invest in a good secretarial handbook. For less than $10 all the information you will need will be right on your desk all the time. My long-time personal favorite is the Webster's Secretarial Handbook.

MEDICAL TYPING OR TRANSCRIPTION

This field is opening up more and more for the home-based typist. You can do such things as: filling out health insurance claim forms; transcribing medical reports; preparing case studies for doctors, surgeons, dentists, or orthodontists to present at their annual meetings; transcribing pathology reports for clinical laboratories; preparing consulting reports for neurologists, psychologists, surgeons, physical therapists, and helping medical/dental offices with overload work.

If you have any experience in the medical field, even if it isn't office experience, knowing the terminology will be invaluable. You can use that knowledge to set up a traditional medical typing service by applying the ideas I just presented, or you can use it in other ways. Because of my combined medical and academic background, I had two very interesting customers.

One man puts on continuing-education seminars for nurses and dentists. Four times a year he needs to have a course outline and a syllabus typed. Because so much of the language is medically technical and because it has to be approved by an education board, he brought it to me instead of to a general business typist. And because I don't enjoy routine correspondence and general business work, he doesn't bring that sort of work to me. He used two home-based typists, and we were all happy with the arrangement.

Another very fascinating job I did was to prepare a newsletter/journal for an association of histotechnologists (highly specialized lab technicians). The president of the association was a woman who had worked across the hall from me when I worked at the university's medical school. She remembered me and my business (and my reputation on the job) when it was her turn to put out the newsletter.

In addition to paying me for preparing the journal, I was encouraged to put a small ad in one issue.

That ad produced a dozen new customers, most of whom were working on their own post-graduate school projects. Before long, the word was spreading throughout that local chapter that I was THE typist who could be relied on to be on-time and accurate. Soon, those new customers were referring other people they worked with. See how things snowball? And me in Southern California without a shovel!

From the research I've done, and in my own experience, you have to prove yourself and your skills a little more in this area in order to get customers. A majority of medical and dental offices are justifiably reluctant to sub-contract work out of their office. Doing so to the wrong person could seriously violate the confidential doctor/patient relationship. You must reassure them that you are confidential, dependable, and accurate. Ask them to consider that having you do the work in the confines of your home (an extra plus here if you live alone) is no different -- and perhaps better -- than their hiring an employee to work in their own office. Once you get the work, you'll get more. Your reputation will spread quickly, so make sure it's spotless.

LEGAL TYPING OR TRANSCRIPTION

If you've acquired any legal experience you'll be marketable in a home-based typing business that specializes in legal documents or transcription. According to my research, this is one area in which you must have prior experience in order to be successful at it at home.

If you don't have the experience, the only alternative I have uncovered is to offer yourself as an apprentice at an established office in order to learn the forms, the terminology, and the method of preparation.

If you have solid experience, you should be able to do very well with a home-based business. A woman in Los Angeles types for two attorneys who just passed the bar. Neither of them can afford a full-time qualified legal secretary, nor do they have the workload to justify one. She has plenty of work, though, by working for the three of them. The three attorneys share a small office that is staffed by a receptionist, and the secretary works from home. Once a week she meets with them to go over any special problems or discuss deadlines. Occasionally she has a "rush" job, but she usually works at a leisurely pace that suits her own wishes. Because she has some limited bookkeeping experience, she does their customer billing as well. They appreciate her, and she is happy with the control she has over her own hours and working conditions.

Another possibility in this field is helping already-established law offices and legal typing services with overload. If you are good, many firms will be very glad to have high-quality reliable temporary help. If you have a lot of experience, you might also enjoy offering "set-up" services to new attorneys who are opening new practices. Organize their files, start their bookkeeping system, order their office equipment.

One more outlet for your talents is transcribing the notes of court reporters and deposition services. A good deal of this work is often done on weekends or in the evening hours which makes it an ideal second job for someone who is already working but needs to moonlight, or an ideal job for a single mother who must work while her youngsters sleep or play.

In most cases you will type from dictated notes. If, however, you can read the reporter's notes, you will make almost twice as much. A woman in Pittsburgh, Pennsylvania, reports that she makes over $20 an hour doing court transcription. You can work for individual reporters on a contractual basis, or you can work for a court reporting service.

Unfortunately, this isn't always the highest-paying work you'll find. In most areas of the country, reporters pay a pitiful 50¢ to 75¢ a page for transcribing from their dictated notes. The work must often be done overnight, for not usually much of a bonus. In addition, if you type from actual courtroom or deposition tapes, people's speech patterns make understanding some of the words almost impossible.

The only way to make acceptable money at court transcribing is to be <u>VERY</u> fast or to be able to read reporters' notes. If you can read their notes without their having to dictate -- that is, if you help them eliminate a time consuming step in the process -- the pay rate per page is at least double in most areas of the country. Even at double the rate, the pay is still low when compared to other forms of typing at home. There are a few consolations, however. Many reporters and/or court procedures specify that the transcribed pages be typed in 9-pitch (9 letters to an inch), and many of the pages are only 24 or 25 lines long and these lines may contain fewer than ten words.

TYPING FOR PROFESSIONAL WRITERS

The final major market for the home typist is the large number of writers and poets in this country. Publishing trade magazines estimate that there are over seven million people in the country who are trying to break into print, either for the print medium or for television, radio, or film. These can range from the poet to the textbook writer, from the novelist to the how-to or cookbook author, from a writer of radio ad copy to a television writer or playwright or screenwriter and everything in between. An audience that large may account for the fact that WRITER'S MARKET was the #1 best-selling non-fiction book in the U.S. in 1979 and continues to be a big seller year after year.

This kind of typing is probably the easiest to do. There are very few rules to follow, and they rarely change. The only ones I know of are:

1. Always double-space (unless an editor specifies triple-space). On the average, a page will have 26 or 27 lines. NEVER prepare a manuscript (other than recipes or poems) single-spaced, and don't use space-and-a-half, either.

2. Always keep a consistent margin on all four sides. (That helps to estimate word count which is important.) Generally-accepted margins are LEFT, 1-1/2 inch; RIGHT, TOP, and BOTTOM, 1 inch.

3. Don't hyphenate words at the end of a line. Go to a new line instead. If a manuscript goes straight to a typesetter, most of them put in all hyphens as permanent rather than as optional. Correcting a typeset manuscript for unwanted hyphens is a giant pain in the neck, not to mention a waste of time and money.

4. Paper should be 20 lb. bond, mimeo or xerographic paper is fine. Some writers may prepare their manuscript on 16 lb. tissue-like paper, but an editor would never accept this. Cotton-content ("rag-content") paper is not

as important anymore with the advent of the copy machine. But erasable paper is a definite taboo! The very feature of this paper that makes it attractive to a novice typist, i.e., its ease of erasure, makes it a nightmare to an editor. The ink smudges and wipes off, and in addition, the high sheen produces an unbearable glare under fluorescent lights.

5. Pica type is almost universally preferred, and make sure you use a standard typeface. Fancy typefaces spell almost certain rejection of the writer's manuscript.

6. Paragraphs are indented five or six spaces according to author or publisher preference. If a manuscript contains any long indented paragraphs (long quotes or special interviews) these are still double-spaced, but within indented margins which are honored even if the paragraph extends beyond the one page on which it began.

7. Film and television scripts and play scripts follow a very precise and very different format. If you're not familiar with the format, ask your client to bring you a sample.

Writers are usually very precise individuals who don't need spelling and grammar help. (Even if some do need help, they prefer to have a typist copy their work exactly, making no changes.) So, you may not use your editing skills when working for writers.

One caution -- from personal observation, and strictly my own opinion, so please don't send me hate letters -- some writers are very impressed with the fact that they are writers, particularly novelists and poets. They are in love with the cultural aura that surrounds them. They consider themselves several cuts above the plebian typist. If you encounter this attitude and don't care for it, you WILL NOT change the writer. Better to bend a little if you can, or, if you can't, refer the writer to another typist who doesn't mind being treated as a subordinate.

In all fairness, many writers, especially the seasoned professionals, recognize that a competent and caring typist will make their writing work so much easier and will ensure that the finished manuscript reflects top-quality skill, for the writer and the typist. A writer-client who fits this mold is one you wish you could clone.

Another advantage to the home-based typist who does this kind of work is that distance from a customer is not always a problem. Very often a writer will send his or her rough manuscript material through the mail or via United Parcel Service (UPS). The typist uses the same method to return the finished copy to the writer. In this way, a home-based typist in a rural area can still make a good living by offering high-quality work with fast turn-around time at a reasonable price.

Another caution note: an attorney friend advises that you NEVER accept a personal check from an unknown by-mail client. Ask for cashier's checks or money orders. Once you have established an on-going business relationship with this long-distance client, then you may revert to personal checks. This policy should be clearly written out, and signed by both you and the client, before you begin work on a long-distance project. More on this subject in the chapter, "Customers."

SUMMARY

I've explored what I feel are the five major markets for the home-based typing business: academic, medical, business/commercial, legal, and professional writers. I believe that by combining your skills with the available market where you live, you can be successful and happy in your business.

When looking at your skills and the potential market, consider anything that is special about you -- anything that sets you apart from your neighbor or co-worker. And don't be discouraged by any circumstance, any situation, or any perceived lack of skill or availability. Look for lemonade in every bushel of lemons. For instance, if you are physically handicapped (or if a member of your family is), turn that disability into a desirability. Consider how valuable a deaf typist is to the millions of deaf customers who are unable to communicate with hearing typists.

As another example, a woman in a wheelchair can be invaluable as an editor to an able-bodied writer who is preparing an article for a handicapped magazine.

Retired teachers and librarians could be booked
months in advance if they offered research assistance
to graduate students. Consider how valuable that would
be to a corporate manager who works 10-hour days and is
trying to get a master's degree. He or she would much
rather pay a competent researcher who would spend a day
in the library doing research than to cram one more
chore into an already overcrowded leisuretime schedule.
How about combining tutoring and typing? How about
teaching typing in your home?

                    *   *   *   *

     Your skills are much more valuable than you might
think. Match them with a market, or create a market
for them. After all, we didn't need hula hoops until
someone created them and sold them so effectively that
we all "had to have one."

     Limber up your fingers, limber up your brain, and
design an effective marketing campaign based on a careful look at your skills, the area around you and what
needs to be done, and how much time and money you have
to chase down the market. Money, you say? Yes, that
leads us logically to the next chapter in the saga.
Consider how much money you'll need for living and taking care of monthly essentials; for providing yourself
with "benefits" such as vacation, insurance, sick
leave; for buying equipment, supplies, or paying rent;
and for doing some advertising or marketing, by reading
carefully through the next couple of chapters.

MONEY

Money is a guarantee that we may have what we want in the future. Though we need nothing at the moment, it insures the possibility of satisfying a new desire when it arises.

— ARISTOTLE, 340 B.C.

$? MONEY ? $

Money can put all that soul-searching and careful market analysis that you did while reading the first few chapters right back to square one. IF YOU LET IT!

Consider, though, that you CAN begin a home-based typing business for as little as $100 dollars or you can spend as much as several thousand dollars.

By taking note of your available financial and market resources, knowing your credit limitations, allowing for your own "employee" benefits, establishing an appropriate pricing structure, and keeping accurate records, you should be able to stay proudly in black ink from year to year. Paying your taxes on time will keep you out of the grips of the law.

Keep these three words in mind as you look at your money situation: NOW, GO, GROW. How much money do you need right NOW? How much money do you need to GO from day to day and make a respectable living at it? How much money do you need to GROW later on?

GETTING STARTED

As I just said, you can start a home-based typing business with a very small investment. A rented type-writer, a ream of paper, a bottle of correction fluid, a pen or pencil, and a ruler are all you need for a beginning.

There's nothing wrong with a simple beginning. I had only $60 to gamble when I started. In all truth, I couldn't afford to lose even that much, but I "blew my wad" because I had faith in myself and faith in the market for my kind of typing.

My first job paid $19. The next one paid $64, and my third one paid $44, a total of $127 in the first two weeks. I had earned enough to pay back my savings account for the $50/month typewriter rental and $10 worth of supplies, and we had $67 left for groceries. That's not much, but it was a start, and in time the jobs rolled in more regularly and we ate better.

Many people prefer to start on a little bigger scale than I did. If you have enough cash, go ahead and purchase your equipment and supplies right at the beginning.

I've included a couple of cost estimates: one for starting a simple business with the bare minimum; and one for starting more elaborately with a full complement of equipment and supplies. Feel free to use these figures as estimates or comparisons if you are applying for a loan.

The amounts were accurate in Southern California on April 15, 1984 -- just weeks before this book was available on the market. With inflation running rampant from month to month, forgive me if the figures differ when you read this or if the cost of living in your area is different.

BARE BUSINESS ESSENTIALS

Typewriter rental for one month plus deposit	$65.00
	40.00
Rent one extra element for scientific client	10.00
Ream of inexpensive paper	5.00
Bottle of correction fluid	1.50
Extra ribbon and lift-off tape	7.00
Pen, pencil, ruler, paper clips	3.00
TOTAL NEEDED	$131.50

ALL SET TO GO
Money on hand, no loans

Typewriter purchase - "Selectric" type	$1,100.00
self-correcting, dual pitch, 15-inch carriage, 2 elements	
Purchase 2 additional elements for steady clients (Italic, math)	46.00
One-year maintenance contract on machine	92.00
Chair - new	110.00
Desk - used at garage sale	70.00
Supplies at local stationers	325.00
pens, ruler, pencils, stapler, staples, correction fluid, ream of paper, copy stand, tape, 3 x 5 cards, 3-hole punch, paper clips, letter opener, staple remover, box of 100 #10 envelopes, dozen ribbons and dozen lift-off tapes	
Business cards	35.00
Reference books - some used, some new	137.50
Telephone installation and deposit	185.00
TOTAL NEEDED	**$2,100.50**

Here's another approach. Prepare your own
budget/shopping list using these categories:

1.   What are the "MUST HAVES"?

2.   What are the "WOULD MAKE IT EASIER'S"?

3.   What are the "STREAMLINED, ALL SET'S"?

FINDING THE MONEY

One of the first places to look for the money is
your own budget, your own resources. If you were
forced to scrape up $200 in a hurry -- in 90 days, for
instance -- could you do it? Is it possible to hold a
garage sale, a patio sale, a yard sale? Is there anything hanging around that you could easily sell? Is
there any spending habit that could be eliminated for a
month or two until you save up $50 or so (could you
pack lunches instead of buying them out)?

At the risk of sounding a little flippant, if
your refrigerator broke and you needed $200 to fix it,
you'd probably find the money somehow. If you depended
on a car to get to work and it broke down, you'd probably find a way to get it fixed or you'd make substitute arrangements until you could gather the money
you needed. By the same token, if starting your business is crucial to your financial or emotional survival, you'll find a way. I know you will.

I also sense that by now you're thinking, "what
kind of clairvoyant (or busy-body) is this Peggy Glenn?
Who is she to tell me to scrimp and save and scrounge
together the money to get going if I don't have a ready
bank account?" Well, "I" am really at least 300-350
other people just like you from all walks of life and
all corners of this country. I have received hundreds
of letters telling me tales of struggle and coping, and
telling me success stories. I can't begin to answer
them all, but perhaps you can take comfort knowing that
you're not the only one who'll start this and struggle
at it and probably succeed just as hundreds of others.

Look to your own resources first. At the risk of
sounding preachy one more time, if you must borrow, do
it from a financial institution. I've been very lucky
myself with family (not so lucky with friends), but
I've heard <u>hundreds</u> of horror stories from struggling
entrepreneurs about broken friendships or strained

family relationships as a result of loan misunderstandings. I'm not saying it will never work, often it
does, but borrowing money from friends or family can be
disastrous. Remember these famous quotes:

    Neither a borrower nor a lender be;
    For loan oft loses both itself and friend;
    And borrowing dulls the edge of husbandry.
        Shakespeare, 1601

    The borrower is servant to the lender.
        Proverbs XXII, 350 B.C.

If you don't have all the cash, but are comfortable securing a personal or business loan based on the
strength of your existing assets or income, your business plan, and marketing research, do so. Be sure,
however, that you have a solid market to support your
debt. If you have to worry about making lease or purchase payments for equipment each month in addition to
meeting basic living expenses, you may soon find yourself frazzled and wondering why you ever started this
crazy venture. That defeats the whole purpose of self-
employment. Worry and frustration are what you wanted
to leave behind, remember?

The major typewriter dealers have a variety of
purchase plans available. You can rent, rent with an
option to buy, lease, lease with an option to buy, buy
on credit, or buy with cash. On the average, one
month's rental for a commercial self-correcting typewriter is somewhere between $45 and $70 depending on
where you live and how much demand there is for the
machines. Total purchase price on a new machine of the
self-correcting variety is right around $1075.

Some office-machine dealers hold their own credit
contracts, while others sell the contracts to a lending
agency or finance company. If you have a good relationship with your bank, talk to the lending officer of
your branch to see if the bank can offer a better deal
on financing. The same is true if you belong to a
credit union. Compare interest rates when shopping for
a loan.

Credit is becoming more and more difficult to
obtain with each month. The money supply may ease up,
but you can bet that bankers and finance companies will
be very cautious about the loans they write. You will
have to prove that you are a very good credit risk and
that you have a solid marketing strategy for your

business if you are to convince anyone to loan you the money. Your best bet may be to start with a rental and then buy the machine outright once you have saved enough.

One of the biggest roadblocks to obtaining a loan to start a home-based typing business, or even an office-based typing/secretarial business, is that there are no census or industry research standards available for what we do. Bankers know about restaurants, bowling alleys, gas stations, dentist offices, and print shops. But who ever keeps records on how successful we are, how much it costs us to set up and keep going? In many places, folks will simply snicker and say, "Oh, she's taking in typing. Isn't that nice."

A personal note here, a painful one, but one I had to swallow anyway. Two years ago when I needed a short-term business loan for expansion on a special project, I visited my friendly banker. I carefully explained my detailed plan, showed him orders already in hand, and was greeted with a pleasant, "Sure, no problem, come back next Tuesday and we'll have all the paperwork ready." But when Tuesday came, and I was to deliver a check to the printer that afternoon, the banker said so sheepishly, "Oh, you <u>do</u> realize I need both you and your husband to sign <u>for</u> this." I was furious! livid! I'd been in business for over 7 years. This banker had watched my business grow and grow. But, still, my kind of business wasn't something he was familiar with, there were few if any industry statistics to back me up, money was tight, his superiors watched every loan he authorized, and I was trapped.

Fortunately I summoned all the business diplomacy and self-control I possessed, called my willing husband for his signature, and I had the check 3 hours later. Be aware this might happen to you, too. Was it discriminatory? Probably. Could I have fought it? Probably. And won? Probably not, and the delay at that time would have cost me real money instead of business pride. That was also no time or place to throw a tantrum: in a small branch in the section of town where all the Chamber of Commerce leaders traded, at a time when I was seriously considering applying for membership in the Chamber.

You may find yourself in the same predicament when it comes time to justify a loan for a home-based typing business. You may face snickers, you may face "You're going to do **WHAT**! for **MONEY**?" I'm not saying it's fair. I'm only saying it may happen. Be prepared for it, swallow it if you can, get a loan for a "new washing machine" if you must, or get the loan somewhere else if you can.

One possibility that did look somewhat promising was the Small Business Administration's (SBA) mini-loan program for women who want to start their own businesses. I'm not going to explain the program in depth, because there are many, many places where you can find out about it, and the rules change monthly. Call the SBA's office nearest to you, or go to the library and ask the reference librarian to help you find magazine articles which discuss it thoroughly. Your library might even have a copy of the SBA brochure which outlines the program in detail.

Again, as with getting a loan from a finance company or bank, you'll have to present a strong business proposal in order to get approval for the money. The biggest factor in your favor will be your enthusiasm and a thorough business plan. The biggest factor against you is that neither the SBA nor anyone else has much faith in home-based businesses -- not yet.

BUSINESS PLAN

Never heard the term? Neither had I until a few years ago. Basically, it's the words on paper of all the thoughts that have been flying around in your head about your plans for your business. And the words are written in a logical format so that someone else who reads your document, your plan, could understand what you were going to do and how you were going to do it and why you were going to do it. In a nutshell, here's a basic outline for writing a business plan:

        Statement of purpose
        Summary of your goals and objectives
        Start-up plans
        Introduction - what is the business
        Your marketing plan - who and where is your market
        Your financial plan -- credit or existing assets
        Operations - how it will work
        Advertising and promotion plans
        What's the competition
        Who are you and what are your qualifications
        What is your personal financial situation
        What management assistance will you need or use
        Any supplemental information

BENEFITS

You can save your business from financial ruin in case of illness, injury, or disability by subscribing to some form of employee benefit program or preparing your own tailor-made program. As a self-employed businessperson, it's foolish to be without at least a bare minimum of health insurance coverage and disability insurance.

Depending on your family situation, you may not need a separate health insurance policy. If you are covered through your spouse's employer, if your "real job" offers it, if you are covered under your parents' policy, or if you already have some form of health insurance, you're probably sufficiently protected at least in the early stages of your business.

But disability insurance is another matter. Don't be without it. Consider your financial vulnerability if you became ill for an extended period of time or had an accident and were unable to work. What would happen if your assets were seized to pay for major hospital bills, or if you were unable to pay your debts because you didn't have some form of short-term or long-term disability or income-protection insurance.

Through contact with the American Business Women's Association (ABWA), I learned of Support Services Alliance (SSA), a Blue Cross-affiliated firm. SSA provides life, health, and disability insurance AT GROUP RATES to independent or self-employed persons and small businesses. When I reviewed their literature in January 1983, the monthly cost for health insurance for an individual was approximately $55.

Write to either or both organizations at:

American Business Women's Association
9100 Ward Parkway
P.O. Box 8728
Kansas City, MO 64114   (816) 361-6621

Support Services Alliance, Inc. (SSA)
Crossroads Building
Two Times Square
New York, NY 10036   (212) 398-7800

You may also find excellent group insurance plans available through your local Chamber of Commerce. Consider joining for a variety of reasons: exposure <u>for</u>

your business, exposure to other business ideas, opportunities to attend seminars and workshops, and much more -- plus the extra benefit of a group insurance plan. An independent insurance agent may also be able to help you shop for an individual health-care plan and disability-insurance plan. You may choose a plan that allows you to visit your own physician, or you may choose a health-maintenance organization (HMO) that has pre-designated outpatient facilities and hospitals.

Private retirement plans (IRA, Keogh, etc.) are also available to self-employed people. The business-accounts officer at your bank should be able to advise you of what is available in your area. In fact, IRA's and Keogh's are available through a variety of sources. A reputable accountant should have information to help you decide what plan is best for you and how you can work it in with your income.

The public library has reference material on this subject, as does the federal government's consumer information center in Colorado. For a catalog of their publications, send a postcard to:

Consumer Information Center
Pueblo   CO 81009

SETTING PRICES

Charging fairly and adequately for your services is an important part of your success strategy. AND, setting your prices is probably one of the most diffi-cult aspects of this whole business venture. For one thing, you may find that after years and years of being told what salary you would receive and never negotiat-ing for anything else, you all of a sudden find it extremely difficult and perhaps impossible to put a value on the work you do. For so long you've felt second-class and subordinate, and now you're in charge and the headliner act, and where do you start?

EXERCISE #1

One of the best ways to arrive at a starting point for setting your prices is to do this exercise:

First: What is the prevailing wage in your area
          for a mid-level secretary? For the sake
          of this exercise, let's use $9/hour.

Second: To that $9, add one-third, $3.

            This is your "benefits" cushion. All
            business experts these days advise that
            it costs an employer roughly an addi-
            tional one-third to provide benefits to
            employees.
            Now we're at $12/hour.

Third: Now add an additional one-fourth, $2.25.

            That is your "inflation and capital
            improvements" fund. This will allow you
            to weather slight increases in the price
            of your own supplies or utilities with-
            out raising your prices too often. It
            will also allow you to save money for
            buying additional equipment, "re-invest-
            ing in your business." Now we're at
            $14.25/hour.

    How does that $14 an hour seem? Too high? Too
low? Just about right? At least it's a starting point
for future negotiations and "figgerings." From this
initial exercise, decide upon your fair hourly wage.
Remember that you're in business to make money and
you're also in business to deliver quality service at a
fair price. Only your conscience and the going market
can help you determine that critical hourly wage. I
can't give you a standard formula that can be applied
uniformly all over the country other than to have you
use the exercise above or the one below.

                        EXERCISE #2

    This exercise involves adding your expenses and
your monthly income needs together, dividing them by
the number of hours you are able to work, and arriving
at a minimum hourly wage. First let's consider a
single woman with no children in a rented apartment who
will buy equipment with a loan.

    First: Monthly house expenses $850
                (rent, utilities, food)

                Monthly equipment payment $100

                Monthly incidental expenses $250

                TOTAL $1,200

                            48

Second: Divided by available hours (120) $10/hr
          30 hrs/week x 4 weeks

At $10 an hour, this woman will barely be able to make her expenses and exist from day to day. There's no room for any growth, any unexpected money demand, any slow week. She must bring her hourly wage into balance with those guidelines back on page 14 under "Budget Matters." She may find herself at $14 an hour just as in the previous example. She may occasionally be able to spend more than 30 hours a week at the business, but for the sake of this exercise I also decided that she was retired, with a slight disability, and able to work about three-quarter time.

Next consider a married woman with a toddler and a second-grader who plans to spend 20 hours/week on her business; a half-time operation will fit in perfectly with her family's schedule, and after working full-time for a few years, she wants a break. Further suppose that she needs $1,100 a month to meet her share of the household expenses and make the loan payment on her equipment. Divide the $1,100 by an average of 80 hours a month and she arrives at $13.75/hour.

Have you followed the procedure so far? Using these two exercises, or a modification of one of them, or a combination of both of them, do your own figuring to arrive at an hourly wage. Then it's on to the next step in the procedure.

No matter how you price the work you do -- by the line, by the page, by the hour, by the document, or by keyboard time -- make sure you don't make less than your pre-determined hourly wage. For instance, if you figure that from handwritten copy you can type seven pages of academic manuscript in an hour (time to proof-read, too), the "average price per page" for academic typing would be $2. Caution: read pages 50 & 51 about that "page" and when you must deviate from that per-page rate in fairness to you and your customer.

Another method is to determine the current price structure where you live and will be setting up your business; then set your own prices accordingly. Be aware, that "going rate" will be different everywhere. For instance, the rate for typing in Huntington Beach, CA, is probably lower than the rate for New York City, and higher than the rate for Pittsburgh or Boise.

Also consider the going wage for secretarial employees in your area. A study by the Administrative Management Society showed 1983 secretarial salaries to range from a low of $246/week in some industries/areas to a high of $362/week in other industries/areas. In your specialty, in your location, what's fair?

One strategy that might give you an idea of the going rate in your area is to call every typing and secretarial service listed in your Yellow Pages. Call the ones with offices, and the ones that operate out of homes. Unfortunately, because too many people are afraid of competition, you may have to be just a little devious. I don't like to do it this way, and I don't like to suggest that you do it this way, but regrettably sometimes there is no other way. When you call these other services, pretend you have a manuscript that needs to be typed or pretend you have a series of business letters with envelopes. Ask how much it will cost and how soon the job can be completed.

Then take the highest per/hour or per/page estimate and compare it with the lowest estimate. As a starting point, you might consider setting your prices right in the middle. For example, if Fox Business Services charges $22/hour, $4/page, and 15¢/line; and Pat Jackson on Elm Street charges $6/hour, $2/page, and 7¢/line; then you might be comfortable setting your prices at $14/hour, $3/page, and 11¢/line. By being right in the middle, you may acquire the customers who are "sitting on the fence" for either of the other prices.

In my personal opinion and based on my experience in metropolitan or suburban areas, no typing job is worth less than $6/hour, $1/page, or 9¢/pica line. By the same token, I think it's a little presumptuous to charge more than $25/hour, $5/page, or 18¢/pica line. I realize that there are all kinds of function or location factors that may make that previous statement seem ridiculous (either too high or too low), but that's my personal opinion after being in business for more than 5 years and after talking to or corresponding with at least 2000 people nationwide.

Naturally, these rates are based on working from copy that is legible, understandable, and non-technical. Doing scientific, technical, and columnar work is much different and demands a significantly higher level of concentration and skill from the typist and therefore a much higher price. In addition, taking dictation from or transcribing tapes for someone who mumbles or speaks with an accent or has volume changes in his or her voice would also demand a higher wage.

There are reasons for charging sometimes by the hour, sometimes by the page, and other times by the line. There are also reasons for deviating from your standard pricing structure. Let's consider a couple of examples:

EXAMPLE 1:

A college research paper will probably consist of: a title page, table of contents, double-spaced text, a chart or table of some kind, footnotes and a bibliography. Each one of those pages has a different format to it. Each takes a different amount of time to type. Therefore, charging by the page may not work out fairly to the typist or the customer. In this case, an hourly rate is much more reasonable.

If another college paper is a lengthy essay with no references, no charts, and no title page, it will be more fair to charge by the page -- especially if you are typing from already-typed copy. If you are typing from handwritten copy, it's a matter of judgment. Is the handwriting as easy to read as typed copy? If not, if it's so difficult to read that you have to slow down to type from it, then forget the per/page rate and charge by the hour. This is an example of why sometimes it doesn't matter if you type 50 words-per-minute or 100 words-per-minute. If you can't read the job, you can't type it very fast.

EXAMPLE 2:

A business letter with accompanying financial proposal is a standard package for many firms. The letter doesn't generally pose a typing problem (unless you have to correct grammar and spelling). But a 4-page financial proposal of tabular presentations or mathematical computations may take several hours to complete. If you charged $1.25/page or even $2.00/page for a job like that and it took you 3 hours to complete, you'd be robbing yourself! In this case, an hourly rate is definitely more appropriate.

In other instances a per/line charge is more equitable. Firms that complete medical insurance claim forms often bill by the line. Medical transcription is the most common area in which this pricing method is used. If medical reports, pathological reports, or case histories are dictated and then transcribed onto a plain sheet of paper, the line rate works out better for the typist.

When bidding on a transcription job like this, or when quoting a rate on this sort of work, keep in mind that every person's method of dictation is different; some talk fast, some slow. Some customers or firms prefer pica type, while others prefer elite. Listen to the dictated tape, and ask specific questions about the finished requirements of the job before you quote a price. More on this issue in Chapter 8, "Customer Relations."

In legal typing or transcribing, the pricing method seems to vary. Some charge by the line, others by the page, others by the hour, and still others by the document. Because of the wide differences in the sort of work that is done, my best advice again (don't I sound like a broken record by now?) is to call around and see what the going rate is. Then set your prices at a comfortable point for a beginning and raise them when you get a steady supply of clients or when you feel your skills or equipment demand a higher fee.

* * * *

Also consider adding surcharges for pickup and delivery, "rush" work or work that must be done on weekends, corrections, illegible handwriting, illegibly marked-up typewritten copy, copy that arrives on scraps of paper or written on both sides of the page, tapes that are nearly impossible to understand, directions that are unclear or contradictory, unnecessary interruptions, "after hours" appointments, unannounced visits, etc.

As I said at the very beginning of this section, setting your prices will be difficult, and I don't mean to sound evasive on the subject. It's just that there are no hard-and-fast rules or formulas for doing it. Remember to first make the mental switch into an "if they could do it themselves, they wouldn't be hiring me", and an "I'm good" mode. Remember also to keep in mind your minimum hourly wage requirements and your monthly income requirements. Last, but not least, check out your competition and the prevailing wage for a good-to-excellent secretary and set your prices somewhere in the middle based on your skills, your expenses, and the kind of work you plan to do.

As an overall pricing philosophy, if you charge too little you won't earn enough money to pay your bills and you will probably attract a less desirable group of customers. If you charge too much, you will scare many of the customers away. Pick a spot in the middle of the road and then move to the left (the faster traffic) or to the right (the slower traffic) when necessary. Please always remember, though, that it's not a crime to earn a decent wage for good work.

GETTING A RAISE

Raising your prices can, and should, be done gradually as you become more skilled at what you do, to keep pace with rising costs, and particularly if you begin to do more and more complex assignments for your steady customers. Very few of them will object to small raises. After all, "everything else is going up."

Refer back to Chapter 2 under the heading "Budget Matters." Good business sense dictates that you re-examine your operating budget every six months or at least every year. Is your income keeping pace with your outgo? Are you making a profit or merely scratching out a living? Do you feel as if you're working more and more hours and bringing in less and less money proportionately?

If you upgrade your equipment from electric type-writer to electronic and/or memory typewriter or to word processing, your prices will need to reflect the increased sophistication in both your equipment and your skills. It's entirely possible that you'll lose a few customers in this process, but perhaps as you grow or as you change, you'll find that you enjoy one parti-cular kind of work and customer better than another. This is one more reason why you need that back-up net-work of other typists that I discussed earlier. You can refer out the customers that you've outgrown, yet you can be secure in the knowledge that these customers will still have their business needs met profession-ally.

Other customers will stay, partly because their business has changed as yours has, and partly out of loyalty. That's one of the most wonderful features of doing business in America. Everyone is free to choose, and loyalty is okay. It's kind of like being fond of a particular brand of spaghetti sauce or coffee or shoes. If that's the one you like, you stick with it even if it costs a little more, because you are always sure of the quality and because you "just plain like it."

In order to raise your prices, however, you have to feel as if you're worth it. I received a call just recently from a woman who said, "Every time I tell a customer how much I charge, I feel so guilty. I could NEVER raise my prices." Working for the love of it will never buy peanut butter and jelly or bacon and eggs, or pay the rent or turn on the electricity. At the risk of preaching one more time, you're worth it or someone wouldn't be hiring you to do it.

Getting a raise this way -- as the owner of the firm -- is less painful than asking the boss or going through a bureaucratic merit-increase evaluation process. If the market will bear it, charge more. If your equipment is more sophisticated, charge for its use accordingly. No strikes, no working without a contract, no hard feelings after collective bargaining or threatening to quit. Simple! Now back to work!

KEEPING RECORDS

Record-keeping is essential if you are to have any reliable measure of your business's growth and stability. This aspect of being in business is very unpleasant for me. I'm much happier just doing the work and leaving the business details alone. I have all I can do to manage a checkbook for my personal bills -- never mind a separate one for my business. But it has to be done, so if you're like me at all, do it in the easiest and least painful way.

For those of you with bookkeeping and accounting experience, this won't be a problem. But bear with me and my friends who are word experts, not numbers experts.

The basic steps are:

(1) keep track of all the income from the business

(2) keep track of all business-related expenses or money taken out as earnings.

Sounds simple, doesn't it? How much money comes in, how much money goes out, and why, what, where, when. It really is simple, but I still put it off as long as

I can every month. I manage to make a bank deposit once a week, and I manage to pay the bills twice a month, but beyond that, I'm not only lost, but I also border on being grossly incompetent by traditionally-accepted accounting standards. I'm not entirely comfortable with this lack of business knowledge, either. It's a little scary running a business and being so uninformed about good fiscal practices. As soon as I find some time, I want to take a short class.

I've hired a bookkeeping service, yet I still put off reconciling my actual receipts to the checks I've written until just about an hour before the bookkeeper arrives. Fortunately, once I've given her the receipts and she puts them into her computer, I receive a monthly print-out of just what money came from where, what money was spent for what, and how much is left for me or how much of a deficit I ran for the month. Of course, carry-over balances are what allow me to spend more in one month than I earned.

For business projection purposes, I keep a running notebook of my income on a very simple form. I plot this like a simple line graph so I can plan year to year what months will be flush and what months will need help from the previous or next month. On the same graph, I run a separate line (either with another color of ink or with a dotted line) to show the month-by-month expenses as compared with income. By plotting expenses this way, planning an equipment or supplies budget for the next year is a snap.

I also keep a simple log sheet on each customer. On that sheet I record the date of service, the general description of the job, the amount of the bill, and any special comments. When a customer fails to return in 3 months, I send a short note thanking her or him for the business, wishing them well, and reminding them of my hours and any new features. If they don't reply or bring more work within a month, I move the log sheet to the "Inactive" file. Performing this simple chore keeps me up to date on what months were good, what customers were the most regular, and how much they paid me.

That little tidbit probably belongs in the chapter "Customers," but since it also relates to projecting my cash flow, I put it in here because I thought of it first here. That information, like other pieces of advice and/or information in this book, has more than one application. Are you taking notes?

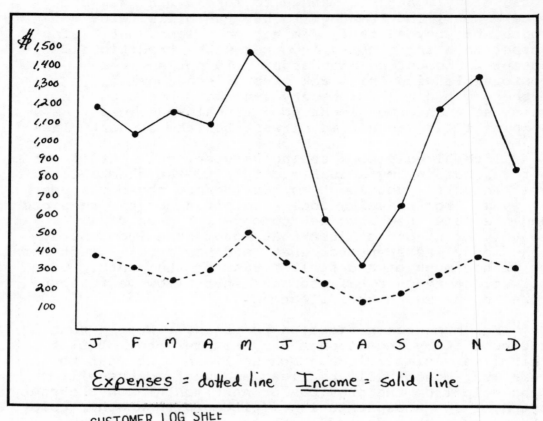

$ 1,500
1,400
1,300
1,200
1,100
1,000
900
800
700
600
500
400
300
200
100

J F M A M J J A S O N D

<u>Expenses</u> = dotted line <u>Income</u> = solid line

CUSTOMER LOG SHEET

DATE   JOB DESCRIPTION

Abby Henc

1/8   Eng. Report
1/20   History of
2/8   Resumé
4/10   Intro le
       & env
6/5   Disserta
9/20   Intro
       &
10/3   Movir

CUSTOMER LOG SHEET

JOB DESCRIPTION

JOHN BURKE

DATE   AMOUNT

2/6   Statements
2/10   E.I.R. (river)   27.50
2/15   E.I.R. (Stone)   85.—
2/18   E.I.R. (White)   85.—
3/27   Consult (Jeffes)   93.—
4/6   Statements   183.—
6/2   E.I.R. (river 2)   27.50
                              106.—

To keep track of expenses, I have a small petty-cash fund that I use for photocopies and incidental expenses, and I use my checkbook for all the rest of the bills. In order to keep the petty cash money separate from my personal money, I bought one of those small coin purses in the dime store (which now sells almost nothing for less than a dollar).

I save every single receipt. I have an expandable file folder which has enough pockets for each month. I match petty-cash receipts with the checks I wrote, and I note the check number on all other receipts. This helps me do month-end reconciliation before handing the paperwork to my bookkeeper.

Now, for those of you with more knowledge of this whole business than I have, keeping your own books is made easy by the availability of several excellent and well-explained record-keeping systems. The 2 systems I am most familiar with are: **Ideal** and **Dome**. Either or both of these systems will be available in your nearest office supply store or stationers. K-Mart carries one or both of them, also.

For learning the philosophy behind sound record-keeping as well as learning the basic steps for carrying out that philosophy, the best book I have ever found for managing the financial aspect of a small business is:

SMALL TIME OPERATOR, by Bernard Kamaroff, CPA
Published by Bell Springs Publishing.

The book's subtitle says it all, "How to Start Your Own Small Business, Keep your Books, Pay Your Taxes, and Stay Out of Trouble!" The book is easy to understand, clearly written, sprinkled with humor and candor, useful, factual, and gives more expert advice than I could ever hope to transmit in the small section of my book that you're reading now. I'm not in the business of selling other people's books, but this one is an absolute must if you're going to operate your business legitimately.

TAXES

This is the part of being in business that I loathe, detest, and positively hate. It makes me "mad as hell" (to quote Howard Jarvis) to give some of my hard-earned money to the government. But I have to if

I want to stay out of jail. (I've heard they don't have waterbeds, crisp celery sticks, or cable TV there.)

So file them I do. The paperwork process is relatively easy for me because I have a working spouse who has taxes deducted from his paycheck regularly. I am able to file my business taxes at the same time that we file the annual personal federal and state income taxes -- the April 15th variety. My business also operates on the traditional calendar year rather than on a different fiscal year (like the government which goes from October 1 to September 30). Even if you start your business in May, you may still consider your "business" year as January 1 to December 31, with five-plus months of operation in your first "year."

Each of you will have a different tax situation. The single woman with no other job may very well have to file quarterly statements of income as a self-employed person. Depending on your income projections and your earnings, you may or may not have to send a check with each quarter's filing. This is your way (courtesy of government regulations) of having taxes "deducted" from your "paycheck" which will satisfy your year-end tax liability.

On the other hand, suppose you're a single woman who types on the side -- in addition to a "regular" job where your employer deducts from your wages. In this case, your tax liability may be satisfied through those deductions from your "regular" paycheck. Perhaps you'll want to claim one less exemption just in case.

Also, because each of you will choose to operate your business differently -- some claiming every penny you earn, some claiming only the checks and pocketing the cash, and some claiming nothing -- no advice I could give would fit every one of you. I know that the "underground" economy exists. I know there are folks who type part-time to supplement meager pensions or Social Security incomes. I know that many, if not most, of these people do not report that income. I won't debate the rights and wrongs of this practice. If this is your way, YOU are the only one who needs to justify your actions to yourself and to any law agencies. I feel that it's completely out of my area to advise you about your taxes -- other than to tell you what you are supposed to do. I'm a typist, not an accountant or an IRS agent. I believe that being a professional in one field is sufficient.

My personal suggestion is to: (1) keep track of all income and expenses, (2) report all income and expenses, and (3) have your taxes done professionally by an accounting expert who knows the tax laws.

If you have any questions regarding the correct way for you to deal with the tax dilemma, consult an accountant for advice. The $25 or $30 you may spend for a consultation could save you from a hefty fine or penalty assessment from the IRS or state taxing agency (if you live in a state which collects personal income tax).

I had an accountant for my income taxes even before I started my business. Now at the end of the year I just give my bookkeeper's printouts to the accountant and she fills in all the blanks on the 1040 form and the Schedule C with the right numbers to keep the IRS authorities off my back. She depends on me to provide her with accurate information, and I depend on her to know the IRS laws regarding what I'm entitled to for deductions, depreciation, etc. We have a good bargain and we trust one another. (We both stay out of jail that way, too.)

TAX BENEFITS/DEDUCTIONS

Yes, there is a tax advantage to working at home, to running a business from your home, and in having legitimate expenses to offset income at the end of the year. Certain expenses that you could never claim if you had a "real" job, are routine deductions if you operate a business at home. For instance, you may legally deduct that portion of the mortgage (or rent), utilities, insurance, and maintenance that directly corresponds to the amount of square feet in your home which is used exclusively for the business. If you live in a home that is 1,200 square feet, and you use 120 square feet for the business (roughly a spot 4 feet by 3 feet), you can deduct one-tenth of all normal household expenses as I just discussed.

Any auto expenses that are directly related to running the business are also legitimate tax deductions. Keep a mileage log in your car and record all mileage that is business-related. At the end of the year, if you drove 25% of the miles for business and 75% for pleasure, then one-fourth of your auto expenses (payments, insurance, gas, oil, repairs) would be legal business deductions.

The biggest advantages to **starting** the business at home, even if you choose later to open an office away from home, are:

1.   you save overhead expenses while you build up your business, and

2.   you are also able to deduct some of your basic living expenses.

It's entirely possible that even though your business provides you with a living, that you'll have a net loss (a paper loss) at the end of the year and be able to receive a tax refund.

For instance, let's suppose that after paying all your direct out-of-pocket business bills, your balance sheet at the end of the year shows a $4,000 profit. That's income. That's taxable. However, using the example discussed earlier (one-tenth of the area of a 1,200 sq. ft. home or apartment), you may deduct one-tenth of the rent. Let's assume $500/month for 12 months for a total of $6,000 and your legitimate business tax deduction is $600. Then you may also deduct one-tenth of the utilities, let's assume another $200 for the year. Total deduction from that $4,000 now is $800. Last, you had $500 in auto expenses that you can directly charge to the business. So your deduction from that original $4,000 of taxable income is $1,300 leaving you with a NET gain of $2,700.

You earned the money, you spent the money, yet you gain the benefit of an additional $1,300 deduction which may reduce your taxable income to a point where you don't have to pay taxes on it at all or at least you don't have to pay as much. I realize that's a very elementary and simplified explanation, but you get the idea, I'm sure.

Again, read the information in Kamaroff's book, seek advice and counsel from a qualified accountant, and read literature provided by the IRS. Take what you're entitled to, but don't get greedy. You'll get caught and it could be expensive, not to mention embarrassing.

Two more tiny tidbits that I've picked up from one lecture or another, one book or another:

1.   If it isn't a deduction, don't buy it or spend the money for it.

2.	Think tax benefits all the time. Read the business news all the time, attend seminars and workshops to learn more.

SUMMARY

I never said how much you can expect to make in a week, a month, or a year. That figure is as variable as there are people in the country who will be typing. Some folks will leisurely type for 10-15 hours a month, others will put in six 10-hour days a week. As a guess-timate, I would say that for a part-time business you can expect to bring in anywhere from $10 to $500 a month; and for a full-time business, you can expect to bring in anywhere from $10 to $2300 a month.

The variable factors are: what kind of work you do, the simple term papers, or technical corporate reports, or translating/editing; what the economy is like in your area; how well you advertise; how many hours you want to work; how you set your prices; what your expenses are; and how well you stick to your budget.

Those income goals I discussed in Chapter 2 under "Budget Matters" will be a big determining factor in setting your prices and in deciding how many hours you must work. On the one hand, if you need only $200 a month for extra money, you can afford to work less than half-time and charge moderately for your skills -- UNLESS you borrowed money to get your equipment and supplies. In that case, you need to make enough money to earn the $200 PLUS the payment on a loan.

On the other hand, if you are setting up the typing business to replace your full-time job, you are probably anticipating bringing in anywhere from $500-$1,000 a month clear profit depending, again, on your expenses. If you were earning $900, bringing home $600, but spending $250 on child care and other work-related expenses, you must now earn about $400 to break even and maintain that 25% cushion.

Once your business gets rolling, there is no reason you can't earn that $400 a month with a home-based typing business. You'll probably find that you don't need to spend 8 hours a day doing it, either.

If your business is highly specialized or techni-cal, you can expect to command high prices while still

working less than a 40-hour week. If you're good at
what you do, you'll be making well over $1,000 a month
on a regular basis.

But the controlling factor is YOU. Not me, not
your family, not even your customers. YOU have to be
the guiding force in the business. You have all those
fancy titles I talked about on page 8, remember? Put
one on and sell your business.

My first two weeks were lean, and I've had lean
periods every now and then over the years. But I
stepped up my advertising, raised my prices a little
bit at a time, and soon alleviated the problem. I
started out with a rented typewriter, a package of
paper, and a pencil, pen, & ruler. The first two weeks
I worked on the kitchen table, and we either moved the
typewriter to have meals or we ate on TV trays.

I continued to rent a typewriter for about 5
months. During that time, any repairs were the rental
company's responsibility. At the end of 5 months, I
had saved enough money to pay cash for the machine. My
first month's rental fee was applied to the purchase
price. When I bought the machine I signed up for a
year's maintenance contract ($52) which guaranteed me
unlimited service calls and parts. I feel that the
$1/week was more than reasonable.

I'm sure that a maintenance agreement costs more
than that now, but the expense is still justifiable.
In a small one-person business, your business must function perfectly ALL the time. Good service for your
equipment is absolutely mandatory. You can't afford to
be down when a customer is on a deadline for the work
he or she has entrusted to you.

I now own everything connected with my business.
As it grew, I used that re-investment money talked
about earlier and added a few items to suit my individual preferences and my customers' needs. I have a
small calculator, a three-hole punch for students'
papers, a ready supply of report covers, a light over
the typewriter, a filing cabinet, office furniture,
some specialized small equipment, etc.

By looking over my past records, I can anticipate
which times of the year will be slow. I put aside
money for those times, and I schedule vacations during
them as well. One summer I took a whole month off!
What job do you know of where you can get a month off

after 3 years of working part-time? I consider my business a success for that reason alone.

I'm confident you can make your business successful, too. But you have to be willing to work at it, and you have to follow sound financial practices. Once your earnings are stable, all this money business will be easy and you'll be amazed at how well it all falls into place.

If you allow for some insurance, follow the business budget guidelines discussed in Chapter 2, set your prices carefully, adjust your prices when necessary, keep accurate records, and pay your taxes, you won't have money headaches. Don't be afraid to pick the brains of the money experts if you get into a temporary bind. Use the resources of an accountant, a commercial banking officer, other women in business, and the reference librarian if you have questions.

Now that you've considered all the "nuts and bolts" aspects of starting a home-based typing business, start writing a shopping list. The next section discusses what you'll need in the way of equipment, space, and supplies.

TAX - A compulsory payment
for which no specific
benefit is received in
return.

— U.S. TREASURY

typewriter..

shopping list

5
EQUIPMENT

You will need professional-quality equipment and supplies to do a professional-quality typing job. I want to discourage any of you from trying to start a typing business with a portable typewriter and some erasable paper.

"Homemakers! Make money with a portable typewriter and a little spare time."

I see red every time I read a paragraph in a book or see an advertisement that screams at you with such half-truths. People (or ads) like that, who prey on unsuspecting homemakers who desperately need to make extra money, are deceptive, unfair, and definitely don't know the first thing about how to run a lasting home-based typing business.

Oh, you may get a customer now and then who will take what you have to offer with your portable, but you won't be able to build a thriving business without at least an office-strength typewriter and a few tools and supplies to set you apart and mark you as a serious, conscientious professional.

THE TYPEWRITER...

While doing research for this book, I discovered that the typewriter celebrated its 150th birthday in July of 1979. In 1829, a man named William Burt of Michigan got the first American patent for a typewriter. He called it a "typographer." A sample from that machine, a letter to his wife that began "Dear

Companion," is on display at the Smithsonian National
Museum of History and Technology.

That early machine was very slow and cumbersome.
It consisted of a rectangular wooden box with typebars
that faced downward around a circle. The "typist"
rotated a lever to a position above the desired letter
then pushed the lever to create an inked impression on
paper. Today's label-makers are a similar adaptation
of Burt's original design.

The typewriter as we know it today (at least the
keyboard layout) was created in 1873 by Christopher
Sholes of Milwaukee. Sholes was the 52nd person to
"invent" the typewriter according to **THE WONDERFUL
WRITING MACHINE**, a marvelous book by Bruce Bliven.
It's worth an afternoon or two of reading. Try to find
the book in your public library. I don't believe it's
currently in print or available in bookstores.

When Sholes first designed the typewriter keyboard, he put the letters in alphabetical order, but
this produced jamming -- especially of the D and E and
the N and O which are frequently used together. There
has been a lot of speculation and historical theorizing
about how Sholes came up with the present keyboard
arrangement. The explanation I like best is that he
put all the letters of "typewriter" in the top row so
that his salesman could demonstrate the machine easily.
After he spread the rest of the letters out in random
form, he added Q, U, and O to the top row to make the
three rows of letters almost equal.

Few inventions have had as large an impact on our
lifestyle as the typewriter. And the machine as we
know it today has come a long way from the original
relic. With the advances in electronics and telecom-
munications, there is no end to the technology and
improvements in a simple keyboard and letter-printing
machine. My using a word processor to simulate a typewriter in this book is but one very simple example. I
have visions of some scientist working in a laboratory
making modifications to our communications technology
as I write this.

Remington and International Business Machines
(IBM) were the leading manufacturers and innovators in
both manual and electric models during the early part
of this century. IBM still leads the field in office
machine sales as indicated by sales figures in alma-
nacs, sales periodicals, and other reference material

my friendly librarian found for me. A quick survey of an office machine catalog, however, shows several manufacturers working hard to catch up. Many offer innovations, many offer lower prices, many offer extra features.

Other typewriters available in this country include Smith-Corona, Royal, Silver-Reed, Casio, Olympia, and Olivetti, Brother, Canon, Facit, Exxon, Panasonic, Toshiba, Xerox, not to mention private labels for the major department stores.

The typewriter has been combined with accounting and computer technology to produce bookkeeping machines, data-entry systems, and has probably contributed significantly to the "Big Brother-ism" and information glut that we have now. For the purposes of this book, however, let's talk about what you need for your business. I think Mr. Burt and Mr. Sholes would be proud of you and me and our entrepreneurial spirit while using their noteworthy invention.

I've already stated emphatically that you need an office-strength machine. I hope you believe me. Beyond that advice, I strongly recommend that you get a new typewriter unless you can find a used one that has been completely reconditioned and comes with a guarantee. A typewriter should have the following features:

dual pica/elite capability

interchangeable type styles

variable vertical spacing
(single-space, double-space, space-and-a-half)

a correcting mechanism

easily-changed ribbons and correction tapes

and a 15-inch wide carriage.

Several companies make machines which have all or most of these features. My research as of March 15, 1983, indicates that they all cost right around $1,000. While preparing for the first edition of this book, I spent about 5 hours apiece typing on each of these machines: Adler, Remington Rand, IBM Selectric, Olivetti, Olympia, Royal, and Silver-Reed. Since that time, Remington-Rand has ceased to manufacture typewriters. Any of them "would do the job" but you need to find the machine that suits your style, your skills, and has the most features for your money.

When I started my business, I narrowed my choice
to the Remington or the IBM. I was looking for a company that could accommodate my financial status as well
as my need to have the typewriter immediately. (I was
foolish enough to have placed ads before I acquired a
typewriter. I already had a customer and no machine.)
I was hoping to arrange a rent-to-purchase contract so
that I didn't waste my money on rental with no possibility of having it apply to the purchase.

The Remington and IBM correcting typewriters were
nearly identical. They were made from the same patent,
as a matter of fact. The parts were interchangeable.
The Remington did have some added features which made
it attractive to me, however, The repeating "period"
key is ideal for my academic work (tables of contents,
charts, etc.). I also appreciate the repeating "x." I
do a lot of rough drafts, and it comes in handy. That
feature is also handy when adding a simple graphics
touch to a page. Lastly, I was impressed with the variable touch control selection and the fact that the key
to activate the correcting mechanism had been moved
just a little to the right and out of the way of the
shift lever. My pinky finger is sometimes a little
wayward.

With all other things considered equal, though, I
decided for the Remington because of the favorable
rental/purchase arrangement, and because the typewriter
was available the day I gave them my down-payment. IBM
had a three-month order backlog and would not loan me a
machine for the interim (unless I wanted to pay their
rates which were higher than any other office-machine
rental business). Presented with those roadblocks,
buying the IBM was out of the question for me.

My Remington SR-101 has served me well for over 8
years now with only minor break-in adjustments that can
be expected on any new piece of machinery whether it's
a car, a typewriter, or a multi-million-dollar computer. But now that the company is out of the typewriter-
manufacturing business, I'm stuck hoping I can find
repair technicians and spare parts if I do have a problem. So far no difficulty, but one of these days I'll
be stumped.

When I bought my machine, I gave thought to the
possibility that Remington would discontinue manufacturing typewriters (as they had several years earlier with
their manual model), but even the giants fall. Some of
the little companies grow to be giants, and some of the

giants grow too fast and have a weak link somewhere that causes their downfall.

On the other hand, one of my colleagues bought an IBM. She had used one in her previous job for over 10 years. Her IBM had always given her good service, she was used to it, and she bought an IBM for her home business. She knew the name, trusted the company's reputation, and was not swayed by any of the competition. Even so, she's not without problems. For a long time IBM stopped manufacturing the Selectric II in favor of its newer Selectric III. She wasn't in exactly the same dilemma I was because there was no shortage of repair specialists or parts, and IBM has since resumed manufacture of the Selectric II. Do you suppose they listened to the thousands of secretaries who argued that the II was better than the III?

An equipment purchasing decision is a matter of personal preference. You must pick the machine that suits your needs. You may have a favorite of your own. The choice of a typewriter has to be an individual one. Look carefully at all the brands: their features; their purchase plans; their service record; their resale value; and the availability of parts, service, and supplies.

Ask for a demonstration and type on each one for 15-30 minutes. If leaving your home for a demonstration would be difficult or inconvenient, ask for a home demonstration. Any salesperson who is serious about selling a typewriter will make the effort to bring the machine to you.

A thousand dollars is a lot of money, so don't be intimidated into making a hurried decision. You are the professional, remember? Salespersons don't have the right to push you around any more than customers do. Before you commit that much money to a piece of equipment that is <u>absolutely</u> <u>vital</u> to the success of your business, look closely, ask lots of questions, and ask for written quotations on price and delivery date. Don't rely on verbal commitments from eager salespeople.

A word of caution about buying a used typewriter. According to the National Office Machine Dealers Association (NOMDA) the "selectric-style" typewriters are the hottest item on the black market -- hotter than handguns. Thousands of typewriters are stolen each year. Many of them are resold at a "bargain" to unsuspecting

individuals (or are they really) who can't pass up a
good bargain. Some equipment thefts can't be traced
because the original owner never recorded the serial
number of the machine before it was stolen, or has
misplaced the purchase agreement on which the serial
number is noted.

Others, though, are traceable through the serial
number. Suppose you send your "new" "bargain" machine
in for repair. Suppose the serial number checks
against the national list of stolen machines? Suppose
you never see that machine again except in court or on
a detective's desk at the police station? You'll be
embarrassed, you'll be out of work, and you certainly
don't need your name in the paper as "arrested for
receiving stolen property."

If you're buying used equipment from a private
party, ask to see the original bill of sale. It's
always possible that if a business is going bankrupt or
has dissolved, you will receive a legitimate bargain.
Make sure, for your sake.

ELECTRONIC TYPEWRITER

What about an electronic typewriter -- one with a
memory? Should you get a word processor? I have mixed
emotions on that issue for a variety of reasons. Even
as I write this revision in March 1983, and as I
reflect on the rapid technological advances of the last
2-3 years, I'm still convinced there is a need for the
plain selectric-style typewriter. Machine sales
figures appear to support my convictions. In 1981,
800,000 electromechanical typewriters were sold as
compared to 206,000 electronics and about 213,000 word
processors of all varieties.

However, an electronic typewriter may one day soon
be the accepted norm simply because many manufacturers,
designers, and repair technicians feel that electronic
machines are less likely to break down than are their
mechanical counterparts. Secondly, and perhaps more
important, is the rapid price drop of electronic typewriters. As their price more closely matches the price
of the standard electric typewriter, the trend may
switch to electronic more quickly. And, as far as I've
been told, when you buy an electronic machine, you may
as well spend a few hundred more dollars for one that
is enhanced with some internal memory and some external
storage capability.

How will you decide? That again depends on that market analysis you did after reading Chapter 3. What do your customers expect? For instance, if I were in your shoes and a lot of my work was likely to be repetitious, I think I'd be inclined to get an electronic typewriter to eliminate the possibility of error in retyping. For instance, if I did a lot of legal work where only the names of the customers change (wills, partnership agreements, etc.), an electronic typewriter with sufficient memory would be a wonderful timesaver.

However, if you were in the academic business where so much of the work is one-time in and out of the machine, electronics and memory probably wouldn't be worth the extra investment. Yes, there are times when you'll have to type a page over to correct a large error, but on the whole, it may be foolish to invest $2,000 or more right now if you don't need to or can't afford to. You can always upgrade later on. Then the typewriter will be a valuable back-up.

If you think your business can support the added expense of an electronic typewriter, and if you are familiar with its use and applications, then by all means buy it. I'm not about to discourage you. As I've said a dozen or more times, **you** do the deciding. What kind of business do you plan, how much work do you plan to do, how much money do you have to spend?

WORD PROCESSOR?

I feel that a word processor is unnecessary and impractical in the beginning of any home-based typing business -- especially one that must start on a limited budget. Most word processors cost several thousand dollars. I would be extremely reluctant to spend that much money -- or to advise you to spend that much money -- until I had a firmly established business with a long list of regular customers who would use the word-processing services enough to pay for the machine. If your budget is tight, I recommend that you start as small as you can, and then improve as your customers and workload permit.

If you have a more generous budget, and a secure customer base, and strong word processing skills, and the ability to market those skills to customers, then your equipment should be a word processor, not a type-writer. The business advice is the same, however, whether you're using a mechanical or electronic typewriter, a word processor, or a computer with word processing capability.

The three best books (of the ones I've seen so far) to read if you are considering purchasing a word processor or computer with word processing capability are:

> WORD PROCESSORS AND INFORMATION PROCESSING, by Dan Poynter. Published by Para Publishing.

> THE WORD PROCESSING BOOK and THE PERSONAL COMPUTER BOOK, by Peter McWilliams. Published by Prelude/Ballantine.

The bookshelves are swelling with new titles about computers and word processors every day. (I have one myself on how to run a word processing business at home, in addition to this one on how to run a typing business at home.) Most stores stack these books alphabetically by the author's last name, so look through the section carefully and choose the book that seems to be written in your style. I'm sure that if I revised this book every six months, I could add at least a dozen new titles each time.

* * * *

The right tools can enhance your ability to do your job. But selecting the right tools is like selecting the right clothes to wear. Any piece from the inside out that doesn't match or doesn't work or doesn't fit right can throw the whole look off kilter, detract from your professionalism, cause frustration, and in this case cost you business. This is no small amount of money to be spending, so use a 4-P process. **P**onder, **P**robe, and **P**lan before **P**urchasing or leasing.

...AND ACCESSORIES

What are the chances that your family will object strongly to the typewriter's noise? If their decibel tolerance is low, invest a few more dollars and buy a noise-reduction hood for your machine. It will cost from $10 to $50 depending upon the manufacturer and the amount of noise reduction you need.

You should definitely get a foam rubber pad for under the machine. This not only helps with the noise reduction, it also provides shock absorption for the

machine and the surface it sits on, thereby cutting
down on vibration.

When you purchase the machine (or when you sign a
rental agreement) also ask about the "bolt-down"
burglary prevention safety feature. This bolt-down
process involves drilling two holes through the bottom
of the typewriter case and through the desk or table on
which it will be placed. Next two bolts are fastened
in place with appropriate nuts and washers. Then the
machine's mechanical parts are placed in the case, the
cover is replaced, and <u>voila</u>, no one can move the
typewriter without taking it all apart. This simple
procedure will probably cost you under $10, much
cheaper and perhaps more reliable than one of the fancy
typewriter-security devices that are for sale.

You should have at least two
different typing elements (the "ball"
with the letters on it). Over the
years I've accumulated seven for the
different kinds of work I do. This
gives me a great deal of versatility. One way it
really has helped has been when I prepared papers for
more than one person in any particular college class.
By using three different elements, the papers looked
unique and not like they'd been turned out by some pay-
by-the-page underground (and illegal and unethical and
unfair) report-writing service.

The standard type faces are:

1.   The Courier style that this book is typed
     with. This makes a clear impression and is
     very easy on the eyes.

2.   This Gothic style looks quite a bit like printing.
     Many businesses prefer this style, and it is also
     a favorite with people or companies that prepare
     technical instruction booklets or lists of rules
     and regulations.

3.   *Italics is used for emphasis or for a more personal*
     touch. This is an example of Italics at 12-pitch.

     Italics also retains its good looks when it
     is spread to 10-pitch. Spread out like this
     it is often used on invitations.

Some other common styles for special projects or
different purposes are:

4. This smaller Courier style is complimentary to the larger one that this book is typed with. I find this one useful when I am preparing tables or charts and don't want the typestyles to be noticeably different from the text of the paper. The smaller character allows me to put more in less.

5. This very spartan Artisan style is also suitable for putting a lot of words in a small space and without having the work look crowded. It is also useful, like the Gothic, when you wish to have a document look as if it were commercially printed. Spread to 10-pitch it begins to thin out.

6. This Elite version of the older typestyles is popular with some people. It is sometimes used to type personal material.
Spread to 10-pitch it is a little thin, also.

7. This Pica element is also a great deal like the typestyle found on older manual typewriters. This element is often used on legal documents.

8. THIS "ORATOR" ELEMENT HAS MANY PRACTICAL APPLICATIONS. IN ITS LOWER-CASE POSITION, IT IS EFFECTIVE FOR HEADLINES OR EMPHASIS. IN ITS UPPER-CASE POSITION, IT IS EXCELLENT FOR PREPARING SPEECHES, BUT YOU MUST LEAVE SPACE. THE LETTERS SOMETIMES MISS, ALSO.

There are many more as well: for technical, scientific, foreign language, and computer applications.

If you _rent_ a typewriter, the contract probably includes one element. For practical purposes, you should rent another one so that you have dual pica and elite capability. My advice is to get the large Courier style (pica or 10-pitch) and the Gothic style (elite or 12-pitch).

If you _buy_ a typewriter, two elements are included in most purchase agreements. In this case, order the Courier and the Gothic styles with the machine, and then buy one each of an Italics and a small Courier-12 style. Buy additional elements as you need them for special projects or to fill a regular customer's request.

The elements cost between $15 and $20 depending on the manufacturer and on whether you get a new one or a reconditioned one. I have had success with both.

MAINTENANCE CONTRACT

Lastly under consideration when buying a typewriter is service. When you rent one, the service will be the company's responsibility. But as soon as you buy a machine, sign up for a service contract as well. The usual warranty on a new typewriter is 90 days. At the end of that time, you need to be sure you are protected against any machine failure. An average service call from a reputable typewriter-repair shop runs $35 minimum. If you've purchased a maintenance contract -- even if it costs you $100 a year. It takes only one or two service calls (with parts, travel time, labor, etc.) and that contract has paid for itself.

At a weekly cost of a little over $2, you'd be foolish to be without protection of your most essential piece of equipment (next to your body, of course). Granted, you may not use it for 2 or 3 years. But consider it a "business interruption" insurance policy. You won't be out of business simply because you don't have the money to pay for repairs on an as-needed basis.

The average cost throughout the country for a service/maintenance contract is $80 a year. IBM charges about $90 right now. My Remington contract used to be $68. Often an independent service technician can offer equal or better service (faster, at least) at lower rates. But, before you sign up with an independent, ask for references from satisfied customers. Call them up and ask if the service was reliable and thorough and on-time. Also check into their loaner policy if your machine cannot be fixed at your desk and must be taken to the shop. And don't allow any repair technician to remove your machine from your home unless you are handed a signed receipt with the company's name professionally printed on it.

DESK & CHAIR

Initially you can "make do" by putting the typewriter on the kitchen table and sitting in whatever chair is the most comfortable. But, believe me, this will get old after only a few hours. You'll be sore,

you'll be uncomfortable, and you'll get tired more
easily. The work you turn out will begin to show all
of that fatigue before long. You'll get careless and
make errors.

You'll also get irritated very quickly when you
have to move the typewriter to eat, and move the dishes
to type. You can get around this switchy-changy for a
short while by eating on TV trays, but why go through
the extra bother? In addition, as soon as you give
your typewriter a place of its own, you will treat the
business as a real one and give it more respect.

My first major purchase (even before I had paid
for the typewriter) was a comfortable, rugged chair in
good condition. I paid $35 for it at an outlet which
sold used office furniture. My used chair held up well
for over 2-1/2 years. When the old one broke a leg, I
bought a brand new chair, and we gave the old one a
sentimental "retirement" party complete with borrowed
gold watch. The new chair has a fabric seat AND back-
rest, a big improvement and something you might seriously consider. In the summer heat, vinyl can be miser-
ably uncomfortable.

I recommend that you get a comfortable, sturdy
chair that will fit your body and your way of sitting.
You'll be spending many hours in it, so be sure it
offers comfort, support, and stability. You can eliminate a lot of back, neck, shoulder, and arm problems by
having a chair that suits you.

I was lucky that my used chair held up so well for
so long and was so comfortable. If you can find a good
used one, buy it. If not, spend the extra money for a
high-quality new chair. I borrowed a typing stand from
a friend for a few weeks until my husband constructed a
wooden platform for the typewriter that was just the
right height and had room enough for the machine and a
copy holder.

I continued with that make-shift set-up for almost
a year. When we moved to a larger house, I had room
for a full-size desk. I found a wonderful wooden
secretary's desk (one of the old oak ones with the
spring-loaded typing stand) for only $50. This gem was
advertised in the neighborhood throw-away newspaper.
Unless the desk will be right in the middle of your
living room, it doesn't need to win a decorator's
award. My used desk is actually quite ugly because of
early abuse and several poor attempts at refinishing

by its former owners. But it is covered with work so much of the time (not to mention reference books, a file stand, and the IN/OUT boxes), that no one really sees it anyway. About once every six months I clean off the top to dust, and then I can't find anything for a week. I'm sure you know what I mean.

A few months ago I moved the whole office set-up from the dining room corner to a now-vacant bedroom. Because I could spare only one day to make the move before plunging right back into the paperwork, I carefully removed all the "stuff" on the top of the desk, placed it on the kitchen table exactly as it had been on the desk (pile for pile). After the desk was re-situated in the new site, I carefully transferred the paperwork from the table to the desk. It was so slick you'd have thought I had just beamed it into the other room a-la Star Trek.

My advice is to get a desk and a chair at the beginning if you can afford it and if you have enough room. Somehow, after I bought the desk my business took on more credibility, it was real. The business now had its own status; it wasn't just something that kept getting in the way or making noise during evening television hours.

When you start looking for a desk, check all the thrift stores, all the stores that sell used office equipment, garage sales, and tell all your friends so they can check the ads in their area.

If you have very limited space (I know a husband and wife team who run a typing business from a 35' sailboat), or if you're disabled and sitting at a desk is difficult, construct a suitable sturdy surface for the typewriter and arrange your supplies so that they are close at hand.

TELEPHONE

You will also need a telephone to conduct your
business. It doesn't matter a whole lot in the beginning whether you use the home phone or get a separate
business phone. What does matter, however, is that you
have a telephone within arm's reach. I can't think of
anything more aggravating than to be in the middle of a
RUSH job and have to get up to answer the telephone 10
feet away -- especially if the call isn't for you.

You can solve the telephone
situation in many ways: add a
long cord to a telephone that you
already have; have the phone
company install an extension to
your present instrument; or
install a separate line for
your business. The choice is
up to you and is based on your
situation and your business
expectation.

For example, a single woman with teenage children
would probably want a separate line for the business.
A widowed woman who lives alone can manage well,
though, with no additional extension at all if she can
rearrange her furniture to be close to the existing
telephones in her home.

Until just recently, we used our personal phone
line for a business line. Initially this arrangement
was fine because our younger daughter already had her
own phone which she pays for herself. I decided not to
get a business listing or advertise in the Yellow
Pages. I preferred to operate my business on a more
one-to-one basis, take referrals only, and see customers by appointment only.

I figured that if I advertised in the Yellow Pages
I would be creating the possibility of walk-in customers. In addition, in order to advertise in the Yellow
Pages, I HAD to have a business line which is billed at
a different rate. I stuck with the residential line
and depended on non-commercial advertising in other
places.

With the Bell System in the midst of deregulating,
all the local utilities are changing their rules as
fast as they can be approved by the state utility
governing agencies. Provided this approach will still

work for you when you are reading this, here is one
sensible way to acquire a business line and listing
without being required to post a hefty deposit as a new
business. There's a reason for this deposit, and it's
as much to protect you as it is to protect the
utility's interests. But, if you already have a residential line, why not capitalize on the good credit
that line has already built up for you? Here's how:

1.   First, order in a second residential line.
     Say it's for a teenager, for a "his 'n her"
     convenience, for your parents, or whatever.

2.   Second, convert one of the residential lines
     to business service. You can convert without
     a deposit, but to initiate service for a new
     business requires a deposit. Why? Because
     many new businesses rack up large long-
     distance toll charges, have difficulty paying
     the bill, fold in a few months, and the phone
     company must write off the debt, thereby mak-
     ing it necessary to raise rates of existing
     customers who pay faithfully.

3.   Next, decide which line will be business and
     which will be residential. Keep in mind that
     in most areas, you may have a dual listing
     (business and residential) on the business
     number, but you may only list personal names
     on a residential service.

Do you understand all of that? If not, talk casually with a service representative at your phone company. Whether it's the Bell System, General Telephone,
or an independent utility, you're bound to find one
helpful service representative who can advise you how
to do this. If you strike out the first time, go back
again (or phone again).

Keep in mind that you MUST have a business service
to advertise in the Yellow Pages (you are usually
entitled to a "free" one-line listing, and that may be
enough for a start). Secondly, you AREN'T SUPPOSED to
conduct business -- incoming and outgoing calls and
widespread advertising -- using the number for a residential listing.

One caution: Don't give away your name or your
present phone number in any of these preliminary discus-
sions. Pretend to be ignorant of what I told you and
just ask questions. Once they pull your record and

you've told them you're in business, they may give you the business. There's no sense asking for trouble until you've figured out your strategy.

The last thing you want is an uninvited "survey" or "just checking" if you've just begun your business and are using your residential line without having converted it to business service. This isn't a jail-time offense, but utilities have a way of making little folks feel mighty intimidated, and who needs that when you're trying to build up a business?

ANSWERING DEVICE

In addition to the telephone close at hand, I recommend an answering device. As you will see when you read Chapter 9, I used mine for ensuring my privacy as well as for taking messages. In the early stages of my business, my answering machine was invaluable for being my "ears" while I was out distributing flyers and handing out business cards.

There are other ways in which an answering device will save you time and worry. My family used it to keep each other posted on individual schedules. With a husband who had on-call responsibilities and three teenagers, for example, just planning meals was hazardous to my mental health. With the answering device, they could leave me a message even when I wasn't home.

A side benefit of my device has been a sharp decline in unpleasant phone calls. It's a sad reality in our world that once you advertise your phone number publicly, you are vulnerable to this kind of rude, cruel, and senseless intrusion. I have found, however, that deviates are reluctant to be recorded and they usually hang up.

In the beginning I purchased a very simple machine on sale at Radio Shack for right around $50. I'm certain the device has saved or made me that much money ten times over. One woman wrote to me and said that she bought a more elaborate model for over $300 that allows her to call in from her "real job" and get her messages. I thought that sounded like a good idea, particularly if you are trying to start your business while still working full-time somewhere else.

Somewhere in that vast price range is the model that will fit your needs perfectly. As with the typewriter, ask for demonstrations, see if there is a trial period available, and shop around for the best price on the model that meets your specifications. You may be able to find a good used model by watching the ads in the newspaper for new ones or by scanning the classified ads and the "shopper" papers.

TRANSCRIBER

In a medical or legal typing business, and for many business/commercial typing services, a transcriber is essential. Again, I recommend a new machine unless you can find a reconditioned one that comes with a solid guarantee.

Some of the models currently available include: Sony, Dictaphone, Sanyo, Norelco, etc. One feature that is particularly helpful on a transcriber is the automatic reverse for 1 or 2 seconds. This allows you to replay one or two words and catch your place in the dictation.

Many models are versatile and can accommodate standard cassettes as well as mini cassettes. This adaptability may be a big plus for your business if you will be doing dictation transcription for a variety of customers. You will be able to do work for the person who tapes a lecture on a standard tape recorder, and you will be able to type for the executive who dictates letters and reports in a small hand-held recorder.

Sometimes you may have to purchase what is being used by the majority of your customers, rather than what is your personal preference. For instance, many court reporters are still using Stenorette machines. If this is your specialty, you'd be foolish to buy a cassette transcriber.

In my academic typing business I received very few requests for transcription. I never enjoyed it when I had my "real job" so I just didn't plan to offer it in my business. Other women prefer transcription to typing from traditional copy. In those cases, a made-to-order home-based transcription service is absolutely ideal.

I don't think that a beginning home typing business needs to include a transcriber UNLESS that business will be almost entirely transcription. Then the machine is a necessity rather than a frill.

If you choose to include transcription services in your business, pick out a transcriber with the same care and good business sense that you used when picking out the typewriter. The transcriber is a delicate and very technical piece of machinery, and should be selected for versatility, dependability, and ease of operation. Once you have narrowed your choice of models, then dicker for the best price, maintenance contract, delivery date, etc.

A transcriber presently costs around $300. This is one item that can frequently be found in good used condition, especially by looking through the classified ads in the newspaper or by buying through reputable office-machine dealers. You might even find one at a pawn shop. If you buy from a private party, ask to have the machine checked over by an office-machine specialist before you buy. If a seller is "on the level" this is a reasonable request and you should have no trouble making that arrangement.

But do be careful. Just as with the typewriter, the black market for this equipment is very active. If the price is extraordinarily low, ask to see the original bill of sale so you won't end up losing your machine to a competent police detective.

REFERENCE BOOKS

A few well-chosen reference books on your desk will save you a lot of hours of frustration. No matter what kind of business you operate, I recommend the following:

    Webster's Collegiate Dictionary
    ___'s Thesaurus
    ___ _k (any one will do fine)
    ___etarial Handbook
    ___al for Stenographers & Typists
    ___ Sabin (Gregg/McGraw-Hill)
    ___lish Handbook: Choices and
    ___ns, by Edward Corbett (Wiley)

                *   *   *   *

F___ ___yping business, style manuals and hand-
b___ ___ The standard ones are:

    MLA Handbook for Writers of Research Papers,
        Theses, and Dissertations

Turabian's A Manual for Writers of Term Papers,
    Theses, and Dissertations

Campbell & Ballou: Form and Style: Theses,
    Reports, Term Papers

APA Publication Manual

American Anthropologist

Council of Biology Editors Manual

A few extras for specialized applications include:

Journal of Biological Chemistry

Biochemistry

Handbook for Authors: Journal of the American
    Chemical Society

Bulletins of the Geological Society of America

Style Manual for Guidance in the Preparation
    of Papers for Journals Published by the
    American Institute of Physics

Journal of the American Sociology Association

In addition, students may bring you specific directions from an instructor. Or a university's graduate
division which is responsible for accepting all theses
and dissertations may print up a set of instructions
that are unique to that institution.

Some of the rules that differ from institution to
institution, for example, are the ways in which you
divide words. In the paragraph just above, the word
"direction" is correctly divided by all the rule books
I have on my desk, but if I had had to divide it "direction" that would have been unacceptable at two of
the five universities/colleges in my area. The way I
divided it two lines above is acceptable in the dictionary even though leaving only two letters on a line
is not recommended.

Become familiar with all the little subtle rules
and regulations by THOROUGHLY reading each school's
guidelines for graduate students and typists. This
preparation can save you many hours of re-typing (which
is at _your_ expense, since it is _your_ responsibility to

know the rules). Most of the guidelines that are issued to students make it very clear that the student is responsible for adhering to all format rules, but we all know that students don't do that. They believe the typist is responsible, so we're all better off if we accept the responsibility graciously and raise our prices a little to reflect that added knowledge and responsibility.

*   *   *   *

If you plan on a business/commercial typing service, you should have all of the books I mentioned earlier. In my reading and searching, I have found a few more which are extremely valuable, especially if you will be responsible for any editing of customers' work.

> The Business Writer's Handbook, by Brusaw, Alred, & Oliu. Published by St. Martin's Press, Inc.
>
> The Dennison Zip Code Directory (available in stationery stores)
>
> Write Right! and Better Letters, by Jan Venolia. Published by Ten Speed Press
>
> The Complete Resume Guide, by Marian Faux. Published by Monarch Press.
>
> Don't Use a Resume, Use a Qualifications Brief, by Richard Lathrop. Published by Ten Speed Press.
>
> Resumes: The Nitty Gritty, by Joyce Kennedy. Published by Sun Features, Inc.
>
> Write Better, Speak Better
>   and
> The Family Word Finder. Published by Reader's Digest, Pleasantville, New York 10570

If your business will be medical typing/transcription, you need a comprehensive medical dictionary as well as a medical terminology textbook or handbook.

> Taber's Cyclopedic Medical Dictionary
>
> The Medical Word Book, by Sheila Sloane. Published by W. B. Saunders.

The Surgical Word Book, by Claudia Tessier.
   Published by W. B. Saunders.

Dorland's Illustrated Medical Dictionary.
   Published by W. B. Saunders.

Physician's Desk Reference (PDR)

*   *   *   *

For legal typing and transcription, many of the
books from the two previous sections are necessary.
The following will also be very helpful for beginners
or veterans:

Black's Law Dictionary

A legal secretary's handbook

Legal Secretaryship, by Norma Blackburn.
   Published by Prentice-Hall.

*   *   *   *

If your business is typing for either amateur o
professional writers, I recommend many of the books
the Business Section and:

Writer's Market, published by Writer's Diges

The Writer's Handbook, published by The Wri

The Craft of Fiction   and
The Craft of Non-Fiction by Knott, published
   by Reston Publishing

The Elements of Style, by Strunk & White,
   published by MacMillan

The Complete Writing Guide, by Carolyn
   Mullins. Published by Prentice-Hall.

Dear Publisher, written and published by Carol
   Shrum, P.O. Box 726, Clayton, CA

Literary Market Place, published by R.R. Bowker.

Complete Guide to Editorial Freelancing, by
   C. O'Neill and A. Ruder

How to Get Happily Published, by Judith Applebaum

                    *   *   *   *

    If you run into any special problem that none of
these books can solve, you still have some options.
Ask the customer if he or she has any additional reference material that can help you with layout, terminology, format, etc.

    In addition, take advantage of the wealth of infor-
mation available in your public library. I know that
I've been giving the library a lot of "plugs" in this
book, but you have no idea how many times the men and
women at the reference desk have helped me out of a
predicament. They have spent hours researching things
with me -- for this book and for customers' work. They
are highly trained and have saved me hours of time primarily because they know where to look whereas I could
spend a whole afternoon just figuring out which book to
look in for the information that I need.

SUPPLIES

    The next best friend that your business can have
is the local stationery store owner or clerk. On a
rush job, having the right tools and supplies close at
hand will make the difference between frustration and
elation.

    Always keep your supplies replenished. Because I
often typed in the evening or on weekends, I made sure
I had staples, paper, typewriter ribbons and correcting
tapes, and envelopes. Post a shopping list right next
to your typewriter so you never run out of anything or

forget what it was you were supposed to pick up at the stationery store.

When selecting a stationery store for your regular purchases, contact all of them and compare prices on a few standard items. Ask if any of the stores offer a further discount to businesses such as yours. The store with initially higher prices might turn out to be less expensive in the long run if it offers a discount to regular customers. Also, a stationery store that offers delivery service is invaluable to you. That service may be worth an extra nickel or two on some items, particularly when you're on deadline.

Build up a good working rapport with the owner or the senior clerk. This will work two ways. First, you will be pleased with their service and the quality of their merchandise, so will likely refer some of your customers to them. Second, they will become familiar with your business and your warm enthusiasm and will send you customers. They will also be very willing to put a little extra effort into obtaining an out-of-stock item when you need it desperately.

The supplies that you will need for a very basic start are:

> pen, pencil, package of inexpensive paper (xerographic), correction fluid, and ruler, extra ribbon and correction tape

In a couple of weeks, or after your first $30 of profit (after expenses), start a list of the things you reached for but didn't have:

> stapler (including staples and staple remover), scissors, 3-hole punch, letter opener, large eraser, scotch tape, paper clips, receipts

With the next few dollars of profit, go back for:

> a copy stand, magnifying glass, more typewriter   _Rolodex_
> ribbons and correcting tapes, 3 x 5 cards or an —
> address book, rubber cement, thumb tacks, scratch
> pads, large plain envelopes, dictionary, pencil
> sharpener, stationery tray for the desk drawer

After you get really moving along and have built up quite a nest egg in your 10% Re-investment Budget, start thinking about a carpet protector for under your chair, a good light for your work area, and a small calculator for figuring customer's bills and your growing bank balance.

An item I added just recently was a desk-top vertical file to separate incoming work from finished work. I use the other spaces for my personal work and one for miscellaneous sheets of reference material.

Would you buy office supplies from a mail order catalog? I would if the price were right and at least a dozen other people recommended the firm to me. There are at least six or seven reputable mail-order office supply firms in this country, possibly more, but I haven't heard of all of them yet. You'll hear from them as soon as your new business name shows up on a few mailing lists, so I won't go to the trouble of listing them here. Addresses may change, and what's worse than writing a letter and getting it back in the mail?

Shopping can be fun when you've earned the money yourself.

6
LEGALITIES

So, now that you've decided this venture is for you, you've identified a market for your skills, and you've solved all your money and equipment problems, you're all ready. Well, almost. There are a few legal details to deal with. None are major hurdles, and not all of them are necessary depending on your business and your local rules, but all of the issues are worthy of note and consideration for any new business.

BUSINESS NAME

Will you be Mary Jones or "Jones Professional Typing"? Will you be "Sincerely Yours" or would you prefer "Speed-o-gram Secretarial" or Sandy Smith? The decision to use your given name or a fictitious name is sometimes emotional and sometimes practical (and sometimes for tax avoidance purposes by using your own name and dealing only in cash). Let's explore the issues.

What kind of business will you be operating and how widely will you advertise it? If you choose an academic service catering to a small clientele for 15 hours a week, you may be more comfortable using your own name. Doctors and dentists use their own names for their professional service businesses. For example, let's pretend that someone named Mary McDonald, D.D.S. sees patients one at a time in her own office and is not part of a large medical/dental group practice. She did, however, incorporate for liability and certain tax reasons.

Suppose you will also be seeing clients one at a time, by appointment, and you will offer individual service as opposed to a large-scale operation. You may choose to conduct your business using your given name with the qualifying, "Professional Typist."

If you choose a business or commercial typing and secretarial service that caters to small or medium firms, you will be wise to adopt a fictitious business name. Businesses prefer to deal with businesses, even though the <u>individuals</u> in those businesses are the most important components. How do you choose a name? Are you creative or location oriented? Are you the "Word Expert" or are you "Broadway Typing Service" whose interest feature is, "I'm a word expert!" Is your location important? "Lakeside Office Services" is probably on the lake or in a neighborhood that is referred to as Lakeside. To a merchant in the area, a landmark may be important. Are you "Tower Secretarial" referring to a local clock or school tower in town?

I can't tell you how to name your business. The process is up to you, as are most of the decisions about running your business. Perhaps these examples have set your brain in gear?

Consider these four simple guidelines when select-ing a business name. Choose carefully because you'll live with it a long time. Changing your business name involves repeating the following processes all over. I know. I named my publishing company hastily, and con-ducted business under an embarrassing and difficult-to-pronounce name for 2 years before being able to change it. Some people haven't let me live it down yet.

1.   Is the name easy to say, understand, and remember?

2.   Does the name accurately reflect what you do?

3.   Does the name limit what you do, or give you room to grow and expand?

4.   Does the name fit you?

*   *   *   *

If you've chosen a fictitious business name (and second and third choices if your first is already taken), now you must record that name in the public documents. The procedure for this differs from state to state, from city to county to parish and township. Start with your town offices, your city hall, or your county clerk. Most business name filings are done on a state level, and business licenses are handled on a local level. If the registration procedure is state-wide, a local agency probably handles the paperwork for the state.

Registering your business name is usually done for one of two reasons (or both). One, to protect the customer. A fictitious business name is just that: fictitious. A consumer must have some way of tracing the owner and responsible person in case of any dispute. Second, to protect the business owner. If your name is registered, no one else may use exactly the same name, and no one but you or someone you designate may conduct business under that name or sign checks made out to that name.

After you've filed your fictitious business name, you must usually publish it. This custom dates back to English common law, before America was settled. Publishing your business name establishes your identity in the eyes and mind of the consumer, makes you legitimate, allows all the world to see who owns "Main Street Secretarial," and proclaims that you are now "OPEN FOR BUSINESS." "Publishing" your fictitious name involves placing a legal notice in a newspaper which receives general circulation in the area in which you will be doing business. The agency which accepts your fictitious name statement will also be able to provide you with a list of acceptable newspapers in which to publish that statement. You are also now on hundreds of mailing lists and will receive at least a wastebasket full of junk mail. Read it all, though, some of it may be helpful or may provide a lead on a new client.

FORM OF BUSINESS

The simplest, oldest, least regulated, and most common form of business is a sole proprietorship. As the term implies, only one person (or in some states a husband and wife) owns and is operating a business. One person makes all the decisions and can terminate the business whenever she or he chooses. This form of business arrangement will suit perhaps 97% of the home-based typing businesses. Tax reports from a sole proprietorship are filed right along with personal income taxes at the end of the year as discussed earlier in the section on Taxes. A tax consultant can assist you in filling in the Schedule C of the 1040 tax return. As sole proprietor, you are completely responsible for all debts and obligations which are incurred in the business name.

Another option, particularly if two people plan to go into business together, is a partnership. Do be careful, though. Friends are great, but they are often poor business partners. Solid long-standing friendships have disintegrated in the middle of arguments over business decisions or money. The tax and banking situations are a little different, and the funds are controlled a bit more stringently. The debts of one partner are automatically the debts of the other.

When considering a partnership, consult an attorney and enter into a formal signed agreement. In that document, clearly spell out each partner's responsibility, authority, liability limit, capital investment, and profit or loss share. Also include the arbitration or litigation method for settling disagreements, the procedures for a partner to withdraw or be added, and how the accumulated assets will be split when and if the partnership ceases operation.

Incorporation is impractical for all but a very few typing or secretarial services. The main reason for incorporating is to protect your personal assets from attack in case of wrong doing or liability. Corporations operate on a fiscal year that may or may not coincide with the traditional calendar year. I frankly don't think incorporating offers enough advantages to outweigh the administrative and paperwork headaches it creates.

The major drawback to incorporation is that the business is taxed on two levels: one, the organization's profits are taxed; and two, income the individuals receive from the business is also taxed. Incorporating your business is also very expensive and subject to endless government regulation. Before deciding on a partnership or on incorporation, consult a tax attorney.

BUSINESS LICENSE

Within a week of filing your fictitious business name you should also acquire a business license in your jurisdiction. These may or may not be the same. For instance, where I live, the county clerk accepts

fictitious name filings for the State of California,
yet the City of Huntington Beach issues my business
license. This simple process might be sticky and might
be impossible where you live, though. I've heard of
some real Catch-22 situations.

Let's discuss the easy, straight-forward way
first. Present yourself and your fictitious name
registration to the business license bureau in your
town, city, or county. Fill out the forms, pay the
annual fee, smile and say "Thank you," and go home and
turn on the typewriter. Oh, that they were all so
simple.

Suppose your neighborhood does not permit you to
run a business from home? Or, you are allowed to
operate a business at home if you don't have customers,
don't allow trucks, don't advertise, and don't make
noise or a mess. In my city, my particular block was
zoned for "limited professional business." There's an
accountant down the block and there's me.

All I needed to do to obtain my license and
permission was to go to another section of city hall,
sign a zoning variance stating that I would not permit
undue traffic or big trucks, and take that variance
back to the business license clerk. There was no extra
fee for this variance, and no need for a public
hearing. I don't have "customers," but occasionally
"friends" drop by, eh?

In a neighboring city, a woman paid $100 for the
zoning variance application, then notice of the variance application was sent to all her neighbors, then
she was summoned to appear at a hearing of the zoning
authority. She was frightened to death until a fellow
businesswoman assured her that it was unlikely any of
the neighbors would object, that the hearing was only
to make the variance a matter of public record, and
that the $100 was the city's way of raising extra
funds.

One other couple in Arizona applied for a license
for their home-based typing business. They were told
that the city had no procedure for licensing businesses
that operated in homes, but also told them that it was
illegal to conduct a business in the city without a
license. This couple was determined to operate within
the law, but finally gave up. One of these days their
city will see the revenue possibilities in licensing
home-based businesses.

As with dealing with any of the utility companies, if you face a stone wall such as this, often the easiest way around the wall is just to hush up and back up and operate in its shadow. To protect yourself, document your activities in a journal or in a letter to your own file, so that if the authorities question you later you can say, "Well I talked to this person on this day at this location and was told this and this." You're covered -- and they're covered with egg.

BUSINESS CHECKING ACCOUNT

Armed with your receipt for filing your fictitious name, you're now ready to open your business checking account. You are not allowed to open a standard business account using that fictitious name until you present proof of having filed the necessary papers. Banking regulations differ from state to state, so the following are guidelines only.

Almost all the business experts advise that you open a separate checking account for all business transactions: for income and for expenses. In a sole proprietorship business, YOU are the primary signer on the account. From my personal experience, I advise adding a second person as authorized to sign on that account. You never know when you'll be temporarily disabled, or tied up with an appointment, or travelling on business. In any of these circumstances, a second person can conduct business for you. Obviously this second person must be someone you trust.

If you have chosen to operate your business using your own given name, business experts still advise opening a separate checking account for the business. Even though the money all goes to one source, you will be able to see at a glance (and prove at a glance) what money came into the business and what expenses were paid by the business simply by leafing quickly through the pages of the checkbook. To pay yourself, simply write a check to "CASH" or to your other checking account.

What kinds of checks will you choose? Those that will fit in your budget and will conform to your style of doing business. For a very limited business with limited monthly expenses and no charge accounts at printers or copy shops, a small checkbook is perfect and the least expensive. It'll fit right in your purse or pocket making it easy to buy supplies without

lugging around a big ring-bound checkbook. For a large
operation that has payroll, monthly bills, a charge
account at the stationery store, and an elaborate bookkeeping system, large checks -- perhaps the style with
a strip of carbon behind the payee's name and dollar
amount -- are more appropriate and more efficient.

Balance your checking account each month as soon
as it arrives and report any discrepancies immediately.
Disputes are difficult to resolve when they're 6 months
old. In addition, you'd be very embarrassed if you
bounced a check because of a math error.

Retain your bank statements and cancelled checks
for a minimum of 3 years. After 3 years the IRS
statute regarding income tax audits expires. I'm one
of those extra cautious folks who keeps the records
just one more year "in case." I've never had an "in
case," but my scout leader trained me well a long time
ago.

ACCEPTING CREDIT CARDS

Accepting payment from a customer via credit card
-- MasterCard or Visa -- may eliminate a certain portion of bad checks, and may encourage use of your services by a starving student who can only afford that
dissertation typing on credit. On the whole, this is a
simple registration procedure. Check with the loan
officer or vice president of your local bank branch.

The only drawback to accepting credit card payments is that the bank charges you a fee, somewhere
between 4% and 6% to act as the intermediary between
you, your bank, your customer's bank, and your customer. The procedure is excellent for dealing with
long-distance writer clients. If you feel that you
would substantially increase your business by accepting
credit cards, do it. If you feel it would be just
another bother, avoid it.

COLLECTING ON BOUNCED CHECKS

Immediately phone the customer when you receive
notification from your bank that a customer's check has
been returned for insufficient funds. If you are
unable to reach the customer by phone, send a certified
letter. All you need is proof of delivery. Don't has-
sle the customer at his or her place of employment, or

call at an unreasonable hour of the day. If your bank
has charged you a fee for the bad check, instruct the
customer to reimburse you for that fee.

DO NOT RETURN THE CANCELLED CHECK until the debt
is satisfied. Occasionally a customer will say, "Well,
just send me back the bad check and I'll send you a new
one." NO WAY! That bounced check in your hand is your
only evidence of the crime, and yes, knowingly passing
a bad check is a crime, usually a felony.

If the customer's next check clears, or if he or
she sends a money order or cashier's check to replace
the bad one, cheerfully tear up the bad check and throw
it away. Errors can happen; they separate the humans
from the rest of the zoo. The customer may have made a
simple addition or subtraction error. The bank may
have made an error. Be cheerful if this is the explanation you receive: and just to be safe, ask for cash the
next time.

SOCIAL SECURITY NUMBER

If you don't already have a Social Security number, this is easy to obtain and will offer the least
intrusion into your personal or business life. To file
for a Social Security number, phone your nearest IRS or
Social Security office and ask the clerk to send you
the appropriate form (#SS-5). You may also do this in
person if an office is close. Fill it out, provide
proof of your birth, and it's done.

FEDERAL IDENTIFICATION NUMBER (FIN)

Unless you plan to hire employees, you probably
won't need one of these. The federal and state taxing
agencies keep track of you very nicely by using your
Social Security number.

To obtain a FIN, complete IRS form #SS-4. Again,
you may do this in person or by a combination of the
telephone and the mail. Once you are assigned a FIN,
you will automatically receive quarterly and annual
payroll deduction tax forms which you must complete and
send back, even if you don't have employees. Why go to
the bother of filing for a FIN if you have no employees? You can't ignore the form and expect the IRS to
know that you don't have employees. They don't read
minds, only paper.

SALES TAX PERMIT/RESALE PERMIT

These two names are often used interchangeably. Unless you live in a state which does not have a sales tax, you are required by law to collect sales tax for some of the services you provide. The laws vary from state to state, so inquire carefully. Basically, services are not taxed, labor is not taxed, but expendable goods, products, or end results are taxed. Most typing services are not taxable, some word-processing functions are taxable, services such as translating or editing are not taxable, yet end results such as graphic arts are taxable. The interpretations of what is a service and what is a product also vary from state to state, so I'm not willing to do any more here than to tell you to check the rules where you live.

As stated before, pretend you are dense and ignorant when you start inquiring. Don't give your name or location until you have all the facts and rules and regulations clearly figured out. Then, if it turns out that you do need a resale permit, change roles and be an in-charge busineswoman who is "here to fill out the forms and get on with the process."

One little tip: when estimating your yearly taxable sales -- only the portion that you will collect tax on -- estimate low to avoid posting a hefty deposit and/or being required to file forms quarterly. Nearly any home-based typing business that collects sales tax will collect so little that the lump sum at the end of the year will be less than $100. Only a small percentage of your annual income (sales) will be taxable (we're talking about sales-taxable to the consumer, not income taxable).

A resale permit also allows you to purchase goods without paying sales tax on them. HOWEVER, you are only exempt from paying sales tax on those goods which you will eventually re-sell in a taxable capacity. Hence the name, "resale permit." Abuse of your resale permit will mean revocation of the permit and possible criminal charges.

INSURANCE

We've already discussed health insurance and disability insurance, now's the time to consider a few more types. These first two may be offered through your standard homeowner's or renter's policy. Ask your agent for details. Be sure to make it very clear to the agent that you want insurance for your business, not for personal items. If you already have home-owner's or tenant's insurance, be sure that any business use or materials or equipment is covered. If you don't have an agent, ask a friend for a recommendation. Sometimes an independent agent is in a better position to shop around and find you the best coverage for the money you can pay.

1. **Fire Insurance.** For just a minute, consider how financially devastated you'd be if fire struck your home. Not only would you lose your home and personal possessions, you'd also be out of business. Fire loss is <u>not</u> certain, it's a maybe. The destruction toll is also a maybe. It could be as low as a couple hundred dollars; it could be several thousand dollars.

   Fire insurance <u>is</u> a certain. For a given premium payment, you receive a given amount of loss coverage. You'd be extremely foolish to pass up the investment and take your chances. Whether you own or rent, sign up for fire insurance -- NOW!

2. **Burglary, robbery, theft, vandalism insurance.** Remember that hot equipment we talked about in the last chapter? What would happen if yours were stolen, if someone vandalized your home and smashed up your furniture? You'd be out of business again, just as in number 1 above. Granted this policy usually has a deductible amount that you must pay before the insurance company pays, but it's worth it.

   I'm going to tease you. Do you know the difference between burglary, robbery, and theft? Attend a Neighborhood Watch meeting in your community and ask.

Theoretically, operating a business from home should be very simple and straight-forward. But just suppose some customer came into your home and was up-ended by a misplaced roller skate or toy truck? Broke a hip? Broke an arm? Sued you to recover the damages from medical bills and acute mental distress and inconvenience? Now you see why you need:

3. **Liability Insurance.** Again, there may be a provision for this in your present policy. Check to be sure. If there isn't, there should be. If you have no policy, consider adding this option when you discuss a complete package with an agent.

If either a fire or a thief (or burglar or robber) forces you to close your business for a week or more, how will you pay your bills and eat? You're not disabled (unless you were injured in the fire or robbery), so your disability insurance won't pay the bills. So:

4. **Business Interruption Insurance** will provide coverage for a very small premium. When planning your total business insurance package, don't leave this out. When investigating business interruption insurance be sure it includes a provision for extra expenses such as immediately renting new equipment or finding a new location and that it gives you enough time to accomplish rebuilding your business. A week may not be enough, a month is more realistic.

Most of these insurance options are plain good sense. Others will be mandatory depending on one or more circumstances. If a bank is loaning you a lot of money, they'll demand that the merchandise or equipment be insured and they may ask that your life be insured. An auto finance company or leasing company will demand insurance as well as protection for their investment until the merchandise you purchased is paid for.

5. **Life Insurance.** One more very important item is insurance on you. What happens to your business if you die? Will your spouse, children, or parents be able to pay off your debts? Beyond that, what happens to your spouse, children, or parents if your business was providing them with an income? Yes, life insurance. At least three times your anticipated annual income (before expenses) PLUS any debt obligation. If you earn $15,000 and owe $10,000, then purchase at least $60,000 worth of insurance. That's a pittance, but it's better than nothing.

That's all. You should be busy for at least a week or so making all the arrangements.

ADVERTISEMENT

Advertisements contain the only truths to be relied on in a newspaper.

— THOMAS JEFFERSON, 1819

Blow your own horn -- even if you don't sell a clam.

It pays to advertise.

— AMERICAN PROVERBS
No date, no known author

When business is good it pays to advertise; when business is bad, you've got to advertise.

— AUTHOR UNKNOWN

If you don't advertise, no one will know you exist. You are your own best (or worst) advertisement.

— PEGGY GLENN, 1982

7

ADVERTISING

Once you have thoroughly evaluated your personal situation, your skills and the available markets, the amount of money you can spend and what prices you will charge, what equipment you will have on hand to start your business, and all the legal steps necessary to begin, the next key to your success lies in effective advertising.

How well and how thoroughly you advertise in the beginning will determine how prosperous you are. You must put a lot of effort into an aggressive advertising program at the start. Notice that I said a lot of effort, not a lot of money. Quality time and careful thought are more critical than a large bank balance. After your initial work, you will probably be able to rely on word-of-mouth referrals and repeat customers. This is always the best kind of advertising, so you want to ensure that your first actions have a snowball effect.

The keys to successful advertising are: be tradi-tional, be creative, and be there -- all at the same time. Translated, that means: follow the accepted rules, then bend them to add something that is uniquely you, and then put your words or yourself where they will be read or seen by the people who will "have to have" what you offer.

The advertising guidelines that I will give you stress the importance of personal contact. That is the ideal way, but by no means the only way. If you are restricted in your mobility, you can accomplish an acceptable level of personal contact by using the mail and the telephone in tandem.

YOUR PERSONAL IMAGE

You are your own BEST (or worst) advertisement.
To many of you, the next paragraphs will seem like
common-sense advice that never needed to be included in
this book. However, in visiting around the country, in
speaking to large groups, in receiving mail or phone
calls from hundreds of people -- I MUST INCLUDE THIS
ADVICE. Too many people don't have enough common
sense, or haven't looked in the mirror lately, and a
gentle reminder here will keep all of us on our best
behavior and looking and sounding our business-owner
best in an environment that won't embarrass us.

A telephone call is likely to be your first contact with a client. Have you ever listened to your
voice? Is it whiny, soft or child-like, curt or
choppy, raspy? Is it smooth, authoritative, warm,
friendly? To find out, tape record yourself, play it
back, and decide if you enjoy what you hear. You may
be very surprised. Most people have no idea of how
they sound. Many don't even recognize their own voice.
Are you pleased with what you hear? If not, can you
change it on your own? Perhaps a speech therapist can
help you identify your problem. You might also enroll
in a public speaking class at the community college.
Try placing a mirror in front of you and smiling when
the phone rings. It's almost impossible to sound
grouchy on the phone when smiling at such a successful
businesswoman in the mirror.

Why does it matter? When you call a friend, you
may not be negatively or positively influenced by his
or her voice. But when you phone a business, your
first and lasting impression of that business is the
telephone contact. You remember if the person you
spoke to was vague or sure, was friendly or rude, was
whiny or self-assured. If you've called a roofer to
repair a major leak, and the person on the phone seems
completely disinterested, you call another roofer. You
have an emergency and you want someone who cares.
Transpose that circumstance to a customer who calls
with an important proposal that needs to be typed.
Will you care, will you be on time; does your voice
advertise that you care and will be on time?

When the customer arrives for the appointment, how
cheerfully do you greet him or her? Do they know you
are pleased to see them? How do you look? How does
your home look? Are things under control or chaotic?
You needn't dress for Madison Avenue, nor look like a

model, nor usher the client into a decorator's dream? The basic requirements are neat and clean.

First, greet all customers at the door with a smile and a handshake -- a firm, but warm handshake. Be on time, even if the client isn't. Be ready early in case the client's schedule changes.

Second, dress appropriately. This means no faded jeans, no shorts or halter or bathing suit, no robe and slippers, no hair rollers, no attire that would negatively reflect on your professional typing ability.

Third, usher the client into a home that appears to have a degree of organization and cleanliness since that is how the client expects the work to be done -- with organization, on time, and cleanly. Leaping dogs, nuzzling cats, and clinging children should be restrained during all contacts you have with clients. Yes, you work at home, but you are in control, remember? If a screaming toddler is likely to be a problem at 4 p.m., then don't schedule client appointments at 4 p.m.

ADVERTISING PRINCIPLES

Trying to explain the principles of effective advertising in a few paragraphs or a few pages is like trying to put someone on the moon using a slingshot. Advertising executives spend years in college learning the psychology of advertising; the effects of color, line, and design; writing effective copy; print vs. radio vs. television; direct mail vs. newspaper.

What I will try to do is skim over the main and most essential elements and refer you to more books and experts for an in-depth look if you need additional ideas or advice.

My favorite theory of advertising is the A-B-C method. All advertising you do should be designed to:

A - <u>ATTRACT</u> new customers

B - <u>BROADEN</u> and <u>BIND</u> your existing customer base

C - <u>CULTIVATE</u> new customers through present ones

When you design a business card, do you want that card to attract new customers, to inform present customers of all of your services, or to be passed around by existing customers who will hand it to another associate, or all of the above?

ATTRACT - If you presented your card to a total stranger, would it convince her/him to use your services? Does it catch their attention? reel 'em in?

BROADEN - If many of your customers are first-timers, you need a card that will inform them of all the services you offer so they'll come back to you with a wide variety of work.

BIND - If you have plenty of business, your card should be designed only to remind present customers of what you do, provide them with something for their address file, and tell them what you do in case they forget.

CULTIVATE - If many of your customers are one-time customers and would not have a need to return, you want your card to be passed to their colleagues and associates (or dorm mates) who would need you. I realize that's a very simple explanation of the application of ATTRACT, BROADEN and BIND, and CULTIVATE to business-card design, but I'm sure you can see beyond the simplicity.

* * * *

Another accepted theory in advertising, particularly with regard to written or spoken copy (words) on a card, a flyer, a display ad or a spoken ad is the A-I-D-A formula.

A - ATTRACT your reader/listener

I - INTEREST him or her by appealing to a need

D - stimulate DESIRE by listing benefits

A - demand ACTION with a guarantee, an offer

How does that translate to a business card? Let's dream one up. First use some interesting graphics, or snazzy card stock, or an innovative lettering style. That's your ATTRACTION. Second does your company name or description identify that you can solve that customer's need. How about "Editing my specialty: typing my love." The customer knows you are the answer to her/his editing dilemma, and also knows you'll care

about the work from start to finish. That's your
INTEREST. You are also "dependable, confidential, and
have 15 years' experience" -- your BENEFITS to him/her.
Lastly, say, "Call NOW for appointment!" There's your
ACTION. The finished product is below.

(Yes, without writing to me for permission, you
may use all or parts of this card. It's my own design,
and I would rather give blanket permission now than
have to answer each letter individually. However, you
do owe it to yourself to try and be creative on your
own. Your own ideas are often better than anyone
else's because only you know yourself and your market.)

Enlarged, this
also makes an effec-
tive 3 x 5 card for
posting on bulletin
boards. In this
way, you can make
one piece of art-
work serve two
functions.

One last tidbit of information regarding what
you'll say in your telephone campaign, letter-writing,
flyer, or business card. A recent study by researchers
at Yale University has identified the following 12 most
persuasive words. discovery, easy, guarantee, health,
love, money, new, proven, results, safety, save, and
you. Use the ones that fit your style and your
business. Could someone **save** time and or **money** by
using you, and are you **easy** to find and will you
guarantee your **proven** work.

COLOR IN ADVERTISING

Fantasize for a minute. What color: is your favorite? motivates you to act? soothes your jangled
nerves? makes you feel strong and powerful? Would you
suppose that those same emotional connections apply to
flyers or business cards? You're right, they do. Here
again, is a three-semester course in a few paragraphs.

Bright colors command attention and/or action.
Red, orange, and bright yellow top the list of the com-
manders. Greens and blues and pale colors have a

soothing effect. Sometimes the combination of a red ink on a white paper with accompanying black or blue ink will give complementary messages.

Certain colors produce almost automatic emotional associations: red with boldness and power, blue with hope and patience (dark blue is authority), green suggests foliage or money, bright yellow denotes sun while pale yellow suggests relaxation or children, orange with either fresh fruit or exuberance. Purple or violet are viewed as either royalty or extreme femininity; pink is also unmistakably feminine. Brown is associated differently by men and women: men visualize wood, leather, some sports; women see animals or perceive stability and ruggedness. Black ink is usually non-controversial, while large black spaces with white ink (or letters reversed from a white background) may mean doom, destruction, overwhelming power.

And you thought you'd just whip up a flyer and take it to the printer and put it on any old paper? Maybe there's a reason why you'd choose one color of ink or one color of paper over another. Now, I'm sure that there are color theorists who would argue with some of the associations and inferences above. Whenever a theory is presented, counter-theories spring forth ten-fold. In truth, the above list is a composite of several schools of thought on color and its impact on human behavior and decisions. If you agree, use some of it; if you disagree, use your own best instincts. These are not my original ideas, merely ideas I've picked up in the last 15 years or so. I've always been fascinated by it and thought it would provide a little light break from all this heavy talk about being in business.

For more advice on how to effectively use color in your advertising, visit a college library or your own library and browse through some of the basic books on color, particularly the sections dealing with the psychology of color and the use of color in advertising.

GENERAL ADVERTISING -- On Paper

BUSINESS CARD

Your business card should convey the impression that you are a professional. The ones on the opposite page are samples of the many ways you can design your card to suit your needs. I'm particularly impressed with

S. O. S.
Shoemaker Office Services
25381 G. Alicia Pkwy. Ste. 304
~~~~~ Hills, CA ~~~~~
~~~~/ 951-0766
Lucy Shoemaker
Word Processing ~ Bookkeeping ~ Calligraphy

ANDERSON TYPING SERVICE

Legal, theses, statistical, manuscript,
resume and business typing

Sharon Anderson
Professional Typist   NE
                            (402)

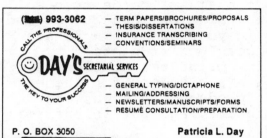

(~~~~) 993-3062

— TERM PAPERS/BROCHURES/PROPOSALS
— THESIS/DISSERTATIONS
— INSURANCE TRANSCRIBING
— CONVENTIONS/SEMINARS

DAY'S SECRETARIAL SERVICES

— GENERAL TYPING/DICTAPHONE
— MAILING/ADDRESSING
— NEWSLETTERS/MANUSCRIPTS/FORMS
— RESUMÉ CONSULTATION/PREPARATION

P. O. BOX 3050
FU~~~~~~~~~~~~~~~~3050

Patricia L. Day
GENERAL MANAGER

STENORETTE & CASSETTE
TRANSCRIBING - TYPING
DEPOSITIONS - LEGAL
STATISTICAL - MEDICAL
BUSINESS - PERSONAL

Travel Arrangements

AIRLINES
CRUISES
TOURS

BONNIE URSINI
SECRETARIAL SERVICE

8700 HUMMINGBIRD AVE.
~~~~~~~ VALLEY, CA ~~~~~   ~~~~~ 968-4844

Word Broker

~~~~~ 574-2017
Res.

JOAN SAUCERMAN
IPTN Member

Professional Typing and Secretarial Services.

D. J. HERRERA
PROFESSIONAL TYPIST

~~~~ 963-5541
BY APPOINTMENT

BUSINESS/PUBLICATION/
MANUSCRIPT PRODUCTION

Peggy Glenn
Professional Typist

BY APPOINTMENT

924 MAIN STREET
HUNTINGTON BEACH, CA 92648

Professional
TYPING
MaryAnn Mack

287-7012

Sharon Anderson's card. The fact that it is typewritten adds to its impact. You can't tell by the copy
in this book, but she has had it printed on very high-
quality textured card stock. It is very effective.

Lucy Shoemaker did the calligraphy for her card.
Ordinarily, this idea wouldn't work so well for a
typing service, but Lucy also offers calligraphy, so
it's a natural. She reports a good response. My card
is actually the second one I designed. This second one
advises "by appointment only," which I found to be an
effective way to discourage drop-ins.

Where will you go to have business cards printed?
Any one of several places, depending on your budget and
the availability of services in your area. There are
several huge firms which produce "boiler plate"
business cards as a service for printers, stationers,
and just about anyone who will take orders for these
firms. The majority of cards produced this way are
acceptable, reasonably inexpensive, and sufficient for
an information-only approach.

One small drawback to purchasing business cards
from a catalog operation such as this is that you may
be placed on a junk mail list -- not by the person you
order the cards from, but by the printer who produces
the cards.

If you prefer to use some graphics or an original
design, search for a graphic artist, design shop, or
typesetting/graphics shop. Check your Yellow Pages,
ask for referrals from printers or from friends. Call
a few artists to compare prices, visit them to see
samples of their work, and be prepared with a few ideas
of your own that you'd like to see someone refine or
expand. THEN, find a printer who will print your
custom cards. The printing cost won't be significantly
higher, you'll spend a little more for the graphics or
typesetting, but you may be dollars ahead if your cards
will attract more attention and bring in more business.

I hate to sound like a broken record, but this is
another of those decisions that will be based on your
financial resources, the creative resources in your
community, and your own ideas in designing a card. I
can give you ideas and direction, but you must make the
decision.

I have a large collection of cards from typists
throughout the country. Send yours to me when you can.

FLYER/BROCHURE

A colorful and informative flyer describing your services is another important part of your advertising strategy. A one-page, one-side flyer is the most effective in the academic or business fields, but can be equally effective in the other three fields as well.

You can post a full-size sheet in most places, but in other places where space is limited, you'll be restricted to a half sheet or smaller. I designed my flyer to be used on bulletin boards, and then I had the lower tear-out sections perforated so that customers didn't need to take the flyer down to remember my name and what I did. One woman wrote that she "perforated" her flyer by using a seamstress' pattern tracing wheel. The task was done by hand on every flyer, but she had the time and saved a chunk of money by doing it herself rather than having the printer do it.

I also have a large collection of advertising flyers and brochures from all around the country. If you're proud of yours, send it along for my file. I may not write you a long letter, but I'm always delighted at the wealth of creativity out there.

When I printed my first flyer, I chose a bright lime-green color to attract attention. As you remember, my market was the academic sector. I needed to compete in the bulletin-board world of rock-concert posters, free-clinic announcements, and homecoming queen endorsements. I feel that the typewritten flyer adds credibility to my work as a typist. I later refined the original design, incorporated a few graphic elements, and still retained the typewritten format. Both versions are shown on the next two pages. Which do you like better?

To post copies on the bulletin boards at various campuses, I first obtained permission from the college activities office. Then, armed with a staple gun and a roll of masking tape, I made the rounds of the colleges about once a semester. I soon found out, however, that I was wasting my time. Competitors removed the flyers, satisfied clients removed them (no one else can have my typist), rain destroyed them, wind blew them off, and janitors were instructed to strip the boards every 6 weeks.

I coped with these developments in a couple of ways. I enlisted a few students to re-post signs.

This flyer covers a standard 8-1/2 x 11 piece of paper, but for the purposes of this book, it has been photographically reduced to fit into the space. You can see in this instance that it's passable. It does the job. Except for the stars and headline, the flyer was done on the typewriter. To achieve the bolding effect, strike over the words several times.

☆ PROFESSIONAL ACADEMIC TYPIST ☆

15 years' experience as university secretary, now free-lance.

Hourly rate includes:
paper, cover, spelling accuracy, help with punctuation,
and editorial help as requested.

Academic manuscripts and formats my specialty.
From freshman level to post-doctoral and faculty.

Will do charts, tables, graphs, etc. No art work.

No job is too large or too small.
I've done it all from letters to reports to theses to books.
Also do scientific papers and manuscripts for professional journals.
References and examples upon request.

Research assistance, library searches, abstracting also available.

Resume development, curriculum vitae, biographical sketches.

NOTE: If you hand-write your paper, use every other line.
It's easier for me to read, so much faster and less costly to type.

PEGGY GLENN   Huntington Beach   **714/000-0000**

= =

TYPING PRO	**TYPING PRO**	**TYPING PRO**	**TYPING PRO**
PEGGY GLENN	PEGGY GLENN	PEGGY GLENN	PEGGY GLENN
HUNTINGTON BEACH	HUNTINGTON BEACH	HUNTINGTON BEACH	HUNTINGTON BEACH
714/000-0000	714/000-0000	714/000-0000	714/000-0000
TYPING PRO	**TYPING PRO**	**TYPING PRO**	**TYPING PRO**
PEGGY GLENN	PEGGY GLENN	PEGGY GLENN	PEGGY GLENN
HUNTINGTON BEACH	HUNTINGTON BEACH	HUNTINGTON BEACH	HUNTINGTON BEACH
714/000-0000	714/000-0000	714/000-0000	714/000-0000
TYPING PRO	**TYPING PRO**	**TYPING PRO**	**TYPING PRO**
PEGGY GLENN	PEGGY GLENN	PEGGY GLENN	PEGGY GLENN
HUNTINGTON BEACH	HUNTINGTON BEACH	HUNTINGTON BEACH	HUNTINGTON BEACH
714/000-0000	714/000-0000	714/000-0000	714/000-0000
TYPING PRO	**TYPING PRO**	**TYPING PRO**	**TYPING PRO**
PEGGY GLENN	PEGGY GLENN	PEGGY GLENN	PEGGY GLENN
HUNTINGTON BEACH	HUNTINGTON BEACH	HUNTINGTON BEACH	HUNTINGTON BEACH
714/000-0000	714/000-0000	714/000-0000	714/000-0000

This version is much more effective with a border around the top to separate the important top message from the lower tear-off section. This border, as well as the press-on letters are available at most art supply shops.

 # PROFESSIONAL ACADEMIC TYPIST

15 years' experience as university secretary, now free-lance.

Hourly rate includes:
paper, cover, spelling accuracy, help with punctuation,
and editorial help as requested.

Academic manuscripts and formats my specialty.
From freshman level to post-doctoral and faculty.

Will do charts, tables, graphs, etc. No art work.

No job is too large or too small.
I've done it all from letters to reports to theses to books.
Also do scientific papers and manuscripts for professional journals.
References and examples upon request.

Research assistance, library searches, abstracting also available.

Resume development, curriculum vitae, biographical sketches.

NOTE: If you hand-write your paper, use every other line.
It's easier for me to read, so much faster and less costly to type.

PEGGY GLENN   Huntington Beach   **714/000-0000**

= =

TYPING PRO	**TYPING PRO**	**TYPING PRO**	**TYPING PRO**
PEGGY GLENN	PEGGY GLENN	PEGGY GLENN	PEGGY GLENN
HUNTINGTON BEACH	HUNTINGTON BEACH	HUNTINGTON BEACH	HUNTINGTON BEACH
714/000-0000	714/000-0000	714/000-0000	714/000-0000
TYPING PRO	**TYPING PRO**	**TYPING PRO**	**TYPING PRO**
PEGGY GLENN	PEGGY GLENN	PEGGY GLENN	PEGGY GLENN
HUNTINGTON BEACH	HUNTINGTON BEACH	HUNTINGTON BEACH	HUNTINGTON BEACH
714/000-0000	714/000-0000	714/000-0000	714/000-0000
TYPING PRO	**TYPING PRO**	**TYPING PRO**	**TYPING PRO**
PEGGY GLENN	PEGGY GLENN	PEGGY GLENN	PEGGY GLENN
HUNTINGTON BEACH	HUNTINGTON BEACH	HUNTINGTON BEACH	HUNTINGTON BEACH
714/000-0000	714/000-0000	714/000-0000	714/000-0000
TYPING PRO	**TYPING PRO**	**TYPING PRO**	**TYPING PRO**
PEGGY GLENN	PEGGY GLENN	PEGGY GLENN	PEGGY GLENN
HUNTINGTON BEACH	HUNTINGTON BEACH	HUNTINGTON BEACH	HUNTINGTON BEACH
714/000-0000	714/000-0000	714/000-0000	714/000-0000

(I offered them a slight discount in return for their diligence.) I placed an ad in the college newspaper. And I did such superior work that word-of-mouth advertising soon replaced my need for active advertising with the flyers. (Please permit me to brag just a little.)

STATIONERY

Unless you'll be sending out introductory letters, you may not need to invest in elaborate letterhead or envelopes just yet. If you're starting on a limited budget, you may simply type your return address on all letters. If you've hired a graphic artist to help with your business cards, though, it may be nearly as inexpensive right now to have her or him also design your letterhead and envelopes so they all coordinate. Then, when you need to use the stationery, take the artwork to a printer. Preparing the artwork is the hardest part. You can print it anytime.

*   *   *   *

Can you do any of this yourself without hiring an artist? Yes, you can. Is there an art supply store in your community? Look through the catalogs of "rub-down" and "lift-off" letters and the catalogs of special-effect graphics tapes and ready-made borders or prepared artwork. Ask for assistance from the clerk. Look through the books for ideas. Spend an afternoon letting your mind shop for ideas and graphics applications that you can do yourself. My second flyer was done entirely with materials I purchased myself. You will be amazed at the possibilities, and you'll be very proud you did it yourself.

SPECIFIC ADVERTISING

There is no way that I can tell you EVERY possible method of advertising in a specific market. I'm sure that if I tell you four ways and they work, that you can find another two or three more that will work, too.

But I will list the most obvious and the most effective methods I know. Sometimes a method for academic advertising will work in medical or legal, and vice versa. Other times a method will work in only one market. You should know YOUR market by now, and you should know yourself and your budget well enough to plan a productive advertising program.

ACADEMIC

1. Hang printed flyers in all appropriate places on college or university campuses. Look for bulletin boards near the library, bookstore, student center, cafeteria/snack bar, dormitories, etc.

2. Go to each separate department (English, Political Science, Sociology, Chemistry, Engineering, etc.) and ask the department secretary to post your flyer for the students and faculty.

3. Find the faculty lounge and ask to be allowed to post a flyer there. Many faculty members, particularly junior members, are continuing their own studies.

4. Visit the placement office, veterans' affairs office, counseling center, research librarian desk, and study labs and leave your information with someone who seems responsible enough to post it conspicuously or file it for easy reference.

5. If you are near a 4-year institution, visit the Graduate Study Office, the thesis advisor's office, and any faculty advisement centers. Leave your information there.

6. Advertise in the campus newspaper. Rates for this are unbelievably inexpensive, and the return is fantastic! Advertising once or twice a week is plenty in most cases. Faculty and students will respond to a well-written ad. I've included a few samples so you can see the variety of ways to write one.

```
----------------------------
|          TYPING           |
| letters, term papers, resumes |
|     Reasonable Rates!     |
|        Call Dalia ▄▄▄▄     |
----------------------------
```

```
============================
|       PROFESSIONAL        |
|          TYPING           |
| Term papers, resumes,     |
| letters, etc. Spelling and |
| grammar included. Call    |
| Claudine ▄▄▄▄▄▄.          |
============================
```

7. Visit all the public libraries in your area and ask the reference librarian to keep your information on file. You may also be allowed to post a small sign on the community bulletin board in the library.

8. If you have an area of special expertise, send flyers to places that employ people in that subject area. Many of them will be taking classes to get ahead.

   For example: one woman's husband is a policeman and she types papers for other policemen who are getting advanced degrees to qualify for promotions. She advertises in all the police stations in her area, and she also advertises in the police association's newsletter. She is constantly busy.

   Another woman sent flyers to an engineering firm because she is an expert at typing technical/statistical papers. She received a lot of business from engineers who were going back to school for master's degrees or advanced training.

9. Visit the purchasing department of the local colleges, universities, and school districts. They frequently need temporary help to process a grant application, or to prepare a faculty member's speech or professional-journal article.

10. Visit the principal of each elementary school, junior and senior high school. Ask to have your flyer posted in a prominent place so that all the teachers will see it.

11. Visit all the private schools in your area, being sure you include any schools which employ teachers with special credentials (teachers of the deaf, teachers of emotionally disturbed children, teachers of the physically disabled). These teachers are almost always attending continuing-education classes to learn the latest developments in their fields.

Obviously, this is a lot of advertising. I suspect that one person could not do the work that would be generated by successful advertising in each of these places. But all of these options might not be available where you live. Pick out what suits your area and your skills, and then put the word out. Be prepared to be busy, and practice your most gracious "NO" speech. You'll need that speech if you did a good job on your advertising.

The particularly busy times for academic typing are: April through June and October 15th through Christmas. The only real slow time I have experienced is from July 15th until Labor Day. This time may not always be slow, either, because a lot of people are doing doctoral study or are attending off-campus programs which are in session all year long.

The slow period never caused me much of a problem, though, because I planned for it in my budget. It also coincided quite conveniently with my family's vacation plans.

BUSINESS/COMMERCIAL

1.   Personally visit EVERY small business within 10 miles of your home (5 miles if you live in a heavily-developed area). Leave a 1/2-page flyer and a few business cards at each place. (My experience is that a full page gets thrown out, a 1/4 page gets lost in the file, but a 1/2 page will find a place on the bulletin board.)

An example of the kinds of places that will be glad to know about you are:

real estate offices   automobile dealers

health food stores   crafts shops

insurance brokers   travel agencies

investment firms   restaurants

accountants   small clothing stores

printers   independent grocers

     designers/home decorators

A real good trick to use in this area is to convince a small-business owner that he or she ABSOLUTELY NEEDS a mailing list or check-approval list. Offer to help compile a list in alphabetical order, using 3 x 5 cards and gummed labels. A good package-deal price for this would be $10 for each 100 names.

This would not pay you a great deal in the beginning, but the long-range effects are limitless. These small businesses will remember you when they need to send out sale notices or newsletters. They will tell their business associates about you, and they will use you to update the list periodically.

Read the literature in the library and that which is put out by the SBA that deals with advertising a small business. Become an expert at helping small businesses with their advertising by using your typing business, and you'll be in demand constantly.

2. Visit your city or town hall purchasing department. You may be a better deal than the temporary agency they've been using, especially if you have any experience at working for a municipality.

3. Obtain a listing of all the service clubs and civic organizations in your area: Kiwanis, Lions, Rotary, Chamber of Commerce, Optimist, League of Women Voters, Moose Lodge, Shriners, etc. Send their secretary and president a pleasant letter informing them of your services and sample prices.

   Make sure that this is the most beautifully perfect letter that you have ever typed. The letter should sell your professionalism and skill even more than the words you write in it.

4. Publicize your services to all your friends who are in business for themselves. Ask them to tell their associates.

5. Buy a set of magnetic signs for your car doors. When you drive around in the daytime, advertise your services. Make sure your phone number is large enough that someone can read it from a passing car.

6. Send a short letter and flyer/business card combination to all new businesses that advertise in the newspaper under "Legal Notices."

7. Use anything from the "Academic" section that might work. This could include visiting a class in mail-order sales or small-business marketing (especially one that is offered at night). These classes will probably be filled with people who would love to know about you.

   It's best to contact the instructor before you barge in on a class. Use tact and diplomacy. Try to point out to the instructor how

you can help the students with their businesses, rather than emphasizing what's in it
for you.

8. Post signs on the neighborhood bulletin
    boards of supermarkets and small neighborhood
    stores. These notices may need to be
    replaced often, but several women report a
    good supply of customers using this method.
    How popular is your local "reader board"?

9. Now that I've got your brain working, what
    more can you think of?

10. Leave a stack of business cards with every
    printer and copy shop. Many women report
    that this is one of their best referral
    sources.

MEDICAL

1. Advertise through the local medical
    tion. Frequently it will provide y
    address labels if you already have f
    announcements available.

2. Visit all the medically-related office
    your area. This includes doctors, dent
    laboratories, x-ray facilities, physical
    therapists, psychologists, marriage/family
    counselors, etc. Leave a flyer and business
    card with the office manager or with the pro-
    fessional person.

3. Contact the local chapters of allied health
    professional organizations (nurses, optome-
    trists, vocational counselors, etc.). The
    work here will vary from typing meeting
    announcements, to preparing mailing lists, to
    publishing a newsletter. If there is a news-
    letter, advertise in it.

4. Contact any medical typing/transcription ser-
    vices that are already in business. Find out
    if they need help with overload. (Be sure
    you do this AFTER you have conducted your
    price survey.)

5. Use whatever fits from either of the cate-
    gories I've already discussed. Remember that

there is room for a medical-terminology background in the academic world as well.

LEGAL

1. Visit all the law offices in your area. Talk
    to the office manager and talk to the attor-
    ney as well. Always remember that you're out
    to save them both time, trouble, and money.

    My best friend is office manager for a law
    firm and says that her firm has two back-up
    typists who are absolutely indispensable in
    times of overload or vacations or sick
    leaves. She says that they would rather use
    these two women than go to a temporary agency
    for help. They are always sure of the
    quality of work they get from their back-up
    typists.

2. Advertise through the bar association by
    obtaining mailing labels and by inserting an
    ad in their newsletter or professional jour-
    nal.

3. Send a flyer to any law school in your area.
    Ask to have it posted for students' use.

4. Also ask the law school(s) for a list of all
    graduating students. Send these students an
    announcement of your services so that they
    can use it once they pass the bar exam.

5. Watch the newspapers for the semi-annual list-
    ing of the names of the people who pass the
    bar exam. Send notices to all who live in
    your immediate area.

6. Contact the court-reporting services and
    offer your typing services. In most court-
    reporting firms, the stenographer is not
    responsible for transcribing the notes from
    courtroom hearings or depositions. That work
    is handled by a secretarial pool or by free-
    lance typists.

    (A little tip: I had difficulty locating
    these services in my Yellow Pages. I finally
    found them under: "Reporters, Court and Con-
    vention.")

PROFESSIONAL WRITERS

1. The current edition of WRITER'S MARKET, LITERARY MARKETPLACE, and THE WRITER'S HAND-BOOK (available at the library reference desk) list addresses of most writers' clubs. Send your flyer and business cards to the secretary of the clubs and ask to be invited to the next meeting.

2. The May issue of WRITER'S DIGEST (a magazine available at the library and on some news-stands) usually lists upcoming writer's con-ferences in every state. If there's a con-ference or meeting near you, contact the con-ference planner and ask to be allowed to dis-tribute business cards and a descriptive flyer during the conference. Frequently you can send a supply of cards and flyers and have them set out on a "Free - Take One" coun-ter. That can save you from having to sit through an entire conference.

3. Two writer's publications (THE WRITER and WRITER'S DIGEST) accept advertising from manu-script typists. Check a current issue of either publication for their different styles, formats, and rates.

   The advertising in these magazines is fairly expensive, and some women have reported good success while others have reported only fair success. It's a good idea to take just a little extra time before committing your advertising dollar.

   Write or call one of the typists who adver-tises in either magazine. Ask how the response has been to their ad. Check with the typists in your area first. See if the bulk of their work has been local people, or people who mail manuscripts to them. When asking a typist for information, please always enclose a stamped, self-addressed envelope as a courtesy.

4. LITERARY MARKET PLACE (LMP) offers free list-ings to typing services. Write to the pub-lisher, R. R. Bowker, and ask for information about how to be listed as a professional typist. (See bibliography for address.)

5. Check your local colleges for courses in professional writing. Contact the instructor of these classes and ask to be allowed to distribute your business cards to the students. The potential is not overwhelming in this area because many writers are acceptable typists, and because still more of them cannot afford to pay someone else to type their work. But persevere; the market does exist!

SPECIAL CIRCUMSTANCES

As I said earlier, much of the success of your advertising program will depend on personal contact with potential customers. However, if you are confined to your home either because of a disability (yours or a family member's) or because of remote location or because of a transportation problem, all is not lost. As a first step, phone a school, company, office, or writer's club. Find out to whom advertising material should be sent. Then send your business card and a descriptive flyer. A week later, follow up with a phone call to assure that the material was received and posted. If dealing by mail, be sure that each piece of correspondence you send reflects the ultimate in perfection and beauty.

If you are disabled and plan to post signs on a college campus or at community locations, ask a family member or close friend to help you. A woman in Tampa wrote to say that she has a post-polio friend who maneuvers around a campus in her wheelchair holding her flyers and tools in her lap. She takes along her teen-age son who does the actual sign-posting on bulletin boards. That's teamwork! A real family effort!

An elderly woman in the next town from me hires a high-school girl to post her signs and run errands. She handles the rest of her advertising by: mailing circulars, talking on the telephone, and sending additional flyers and cards with each customer.

SUMMARY

I've just about run out of ideas (my own and those contributed by earlier readers). Some women have written from various areas of the country to say that they often had to make repeated contacts with some of their early customers. Some others reported that when they visited a business, they took along a portfolio of the work they could do. This seemed to provide good results.

What's in a portfolio? How is it presented? A portfolio should include one example of every kind of typing job you've ever done: from invoices to letters, from poetry to manuscripts, from engineering specifications to financial proposals. DO NOT INCLUDE any confidential matter that would be detrimental to a former client. Always ask permission before saving a copy for your portfolio. Purchase a 3-ring binder and some plastic or acetate sheet protectors. You'll have fun building up a portfolio. You'll be amazed at the variety of jobs you'll do, and the wide range of your skills. You should also be mighty proud when you've assembled it.

If you're just beginning, start a sample portfolio now. For introduction purposes before visiting potential clients, type a fictional letter, a fictional resume, a fictional invoice, a fictional balance sheet, a fictional term-paper page. Preparing this make-believe portfolio will also help pass the time while you're waiting for that first phone call.

If you come up with a novel advertising approach, let me know. Some of the more creative ones I've heard about were:

1.   taking a half-page ad in the high-school sports program (Lots of independent-businessman-football-fathers responded to a professionally written ad in the Homecoming issue.)

2.   offering to do a high school band-booster mailing list free in return for a free ad in the band's Spring concert program (The owner of a musical-instrument store hired the woman to help him keep his instrument-rental records straight.)

3.   designing a "welcome letter" for an independent real estate saleswoman in exchange for having the typist's card distributed to each new home buyer and each realtor the saleswoman knew. (This produced a steady academic customer and numerous referrals.)

I believe that of the five markets I've just discussed, the most lucrative is academic. It is also the easiest in which to advertise. Keep in mind, though, that this is the case where I live. If you live in an area where very few people are attending college, or where there is already an abundance of academic typists and only a limited market, you should concentrate your skills in another market.

Use your market analysis from Chapter 3 to determine what you will do. Then use the advertising suggestions in this chapter to get the most out of your market.

I didn't list a lot of good books on advertising in this chapter,and there are plenty of them. Refer to the bibliography for more information and also visit your library or bookstore to find more that I haven't listed. I will clue you in to my favorites: **HOW TO ADVERTISE AND PROMOTE YOUR SMALL BUSINESS**, by G. M. Siegel, published by John Wiley and Sons; and **SPEAK EASY** by Sandy Livner, published by Summit Books.

8
PUBLICITY, ETC.

AN EXPLANATION

Promotion and publicity differ from advertising in that you don't usually pay any money for publicity's end result. (You may pay to <u>implement</u> a promotion idea, but the process isn't the same as buying ad space or air time or preparing an ad brochure or card.)

By the same token, publicity makes you believable. If a story appears about you in your hometown newspaper, that's tantamount to an endorsement. By being an entrepreneur, starting a business at home as a renegade secretary, or combining the best of the work and home worlds, you've captured attention. That is news. Taking an ad in the classified section of the paper is not news. News is believable, ads are questioned. Ads aren't seen by as many people, and aren't talked about, and don't make you a celebrity.

"Publicity can take the form of news, information or actions designed to attract attention, create interest and gain support. Planning which of several forms (or routes) your publicity program will take is most important. Indeed, this is what a publicity program consists of -- different techniques working together. What can publicity do? It can:

> Increase awareness of programs or services
> . . . and . . .
> Thereby create, build, change, or enhance a public image."

From the Publicity Handbook, copyright by the Sperry and Hutchinson Company.

That's what it is, and why you need it. The public (your customers) will become aware of your services; and the publicity program that you design (one idea or several throughout the year) will create, build and enhance your business image in the public's mind.

To quote the Sperry booklet again, "The first step is to determine what (you) want to accomplish through a publicity program. All subsequent efforts will be based on your objectives. Set long- and short-term objectives."

"The aim of a publicity program should be to reach and influence the public (that is) important to you."

This Publicity Handbook I've quoted from is written for professional publicity directors, the folks who work to create positive public images for large corporations and organizations. But our businesses loom just as large in our own pride, don't they? Last I knew, the handbook was free for the asking. To find out if you may receive a copy, send an inquiry (please again enclose that courtesy stamped, self-addressed envelope, this time a large manila envelope with three stamps on it) to:

Sperry and Hutchinson Company
Attn: Consumer Services
2900 W. Seminary Drive
Fort Worth TX 76133

SO HOW DO YOU DO IT?

There are literally hundreds of ways to create publicity. PROMOTION creates attention, which results in PUBLICITY for what you did. I think the most logical way for me to explain this to you is to show a few examples. Here's a very clever promotion idea that generated lots of favorable publicity.

On National Secretaries' Day, one home-based typist invited all her regular clients to a light buffet lunch that she prepared. Because this was the reverse of the usual "roses and a free lunch" routine that bosses go through for their secretaries, she received coverage in her local newspaper, the radio station came out, and the local television crew stopped by for a free lunch, too.

Now then, buying the food cost her some money, preparing the food cost her a little time (which was money), and sending out invitations to the clients cost her a little time and a little money. But, consider the return on her investment. Anyone who read that day's paper, listened to the radio broadcast, or watched the television newscast knew that she was in business and that she enjoyed it. She says that she received no less than 25 new clients as a result of that one simple idea. How did she do it?

First, she thought of the idea. In an after-dinner gab session with her husband she casually mentioned how she would miss that token free lunch and bunch of roses now that she was working for herself. The next bit of conversation was about how much she appreciated the regular clients who kept her in business. That evolved into planning a small informal luncheon as a gesture of appreciation TO THEM, FROM HER. She figured she'd receive emotional roses -- the old "better to give than to receive" routine.

Second, she typed up 25 invitations to the luncheon using blank party invitations she purchased from a gift and card store. She asked for R.S.V.P.'s and 17 people said they'd show up.

Third, she told a few of her still-working friends about her party, and about how excited she was. One of those friends told her own boss who happened to tell a publicity professional at a Chamber of Commerce meeting. The publicity professional recognized a good story and called the newspaper, the radio station, and the television station (after checking with the hostess first for permission). The rest is history.

You can do the same thing, or any variation of it. If you don't have that publicity connection, do your own. Often just a telephone call will be sufficient to alert the press. How else do you suppose they find out about what's going on? Sometimes you can guarantee results by sending a written press release before, or as follow-up, to that phone call.

Again, as with much of the advertising information in the last chapter, to try and tell you everything I know about publicity, and everything there IS to know about publicity would take a whole 2-year college course and at least two or three good books, and probably 6 months' minimum of working at it. I hope, though, that with this example and more that I'll use

later on, you'll grasp the major points. My absolute
favorite book on publicity is:

PUBLICITY: <u>How To Get It</u>, by Richard O'Brien.
Published by Harper & Row.

How does publicity work? Via the telephone, via
the typewriter, via word of mouth. The example on the
previous page is a nice idea that was turned into a
promotional event. Sometimes it's accidental, sometimes you plan it that way. Ah-ha, you're thinking
already, aren't you?

> One woman, whose business was named The
> Classical Carriage, advertised that she
> would do resumes "by appointment while
> you wait." Then, to avoid being inter-
> rupted while doing the work, she provided
> her customers with earphones and a reclin-
> ing chair so they could listen to the
> local classical radio station and relax
> for a half hour or so. Of course, not
> all customers took advantage of her
> offer, but one day the local music colum-
> nist heard about it and wrote her up in
> the Sunday paper. The manager of the
> radio station saw the item in the news-
> paper, was delighted for the unsolicited
> publicity himself, and arranged to have
> the woman's service talked about on the
> radio.

Promotion or publicity is also the use of give-
away items (freebies, trinkets, goodies) that are
printed with your company name. Pens, rulers,
refrigerator magnets, you've seen hundreds of them.
The term for these trinkets is actually "specialty
advertising items," but the effect is more of a
promotion and publicity gimmick than a real advertising
program. To find a firm that can supply you with these
items, look in the Yellow Pages under "Advertising
- Specialty."

> Another typist gave away 100 orange see-
> through plastic rulers at a church
> bazaar. Why? Her company was named
> "Golden Rule Professional Typing." And,
> of course, she had her business name
> printed on the rulers. She spent an 8-
> hour day at the bazaar and approximately
> $35 dollars on the rulers. Within a week

she had received $250 dollars' worth of
new clients. For another month, more
work poured in and she referred a lot of
it to overload helpers.

Take advantage of every possibility to tell someone (or a whole group of someones) about what you do
for a living. For instance:

Invite yourself to the high school's career day.
If the kids aren't interested, perhaps their
teachers or their parents are. The local newspaper or the school paper might also write up the
event.

If your church or synagogue has a women's group,
ask to arrange a career night where you and
several other women with interesting jobs or
businesses would give 15-20 minute presentations
about what you do.

Offer to teach a class to 4-H or Girl Scout troops
at the high-school level. Office practices or job-
finding skills or business-running skills are
popular subjects.

Whenever you attend a meeting where they perform
the "who are you-around the room-let's all tell"
ritual, be sure to sing out loud and clear just
who you are and what you do and how great it makes
you feel. This can be anything from a Tupperware
party to a PTA meeting to a meeting of the Chamber
of Commerce.

HOW OFTEN?

Why not plan one small promotion event for every
month? You can key to the various holidays or make up
excuses. For instance:

JANUARY -- "Start the new year right by having ABC
Secretarial do your resume."

FEBRUARY -- "I LOVE all my customers." Happy
Valentine's Day cards are great reminders. "I cannot
tell a lie. I'm the best there is." Washington's
Birthday hype.

MARCH -- cold? blustery? miserable? how 'bout
asking all customers to stop for a hot cup of tea when

127

they bring their work?   anniversary for your business?
St. Patrick's Day party?

APRIL -- raining? Easter eggs? Christian theme?
Passover? spring break? Secretaries' Day? first day
of Spring?

MAY -- when was the last time you received a May
basket from a secret admirer? Could you design a "May
basket" flyer with benefits written in each flower?

JUNE -- graduation notices for all the students
who survived? anybody getting married or celebrating
an anniversary?

JULY -- Independence Day, the country's and
your's, too; serve iced tea to cool off those customers
who were freezing in March?

AUGUST -- this month is yours, how 'bout a
vacation special, a back-to-school sale with 10% off
every order over $25?

SEPTEMBER -- Labor Day, back-to-school again,
Jewish holidays

OCTOBER -- Columbus discovered America, you
discovered the joy of self-employment and your special
clients; Halloween

NOVEMBER -- Election Day, cast your vote for your
favorite freelance typist/secretary; Thanksgiving,
maybe a better time to send greetings than next month
when so many will be competing for attention

DECEMBER -- snow sale? Christmas special?
Hanukkah special? end-of-the-year clearance?

Now your mind is really whirring, isn't it? And
you thought this whole thing was so easy? It is easy!
And it's fun! And you're the boss! You're in control!

SUMMARY

This is a short chapter, but the information
didn't seem to fit logically anywhere else. I could go
on for pages and pages, but then all you would have are
my ideas and none of your own. Besides, my brain does
run dry after a while, honest. Try to perform one

simple promotion or publicity function a week. Call up a client you haven't heard from in a while, work on a new flyer for an event or stunt next month, tell just one new person about what you do, drop a stack of business cards at just one more printer or copy shop.

The limits to a successful promotion and publicity program don't exist. There are no limits to your talent, your creativity, your drive to make a go of this. Of course, if you already have more work than you can handle, we'll forgive you. You may stay glued to the chair and keyboard until you catch up. But, as soon as it drops off, back you go to the monthly plan. No worrying or whining allowed. It doesn't fit that image you've just created. Find something to do, don't spend much money on it, but do spend some time and thought on it. And have fun!

PERSISTENCE with your PROMOTION and PUBLICITY will PRODUCE a PUBLIC image that will result in PROFITS.

* * * *

P.S. Whatever positive publicity you receive is positive publicity for the whole profession -- for everyone else who works at home with a typewriter or word processor, for every secretary everywhere. Publicity and promotion are ways to get the world to stand up and recognize that there is great dignity in working with words, a keyboard, and paper.

We're artists. It takes a special skill to turn out a clean manuscript, a crisp letter with uniform margins and balance on the page, a financial proposal with straight columns, a commanding resume that helps someone land a new job. We have that skill and we want everyone to know it, respect us for it, and pay us well for it.

Please.
Thank you.
You're welcome.

How soon?　　How much?

9
CUSTOMERS

A home-based typing business depends upon customers. A SUCCESSFUL home-based typing business depends upon EFFECTIVE CUSTOMER RELATIONS -- public relations.

Businesses lose customers primarily because of personality conflicts or emotional reasons -- not because of poor workmanship. Most businesses don't do shoddy work. Getting along with your customers, and making sure they get along with you requires some pre-planning.

The time to decide on your business' general policies and procedures is now, before you have to "think on your feet." What is your policy on deposits for large orders, on checks or cash, on who fixes errors, on being asked to do something that may be unethical or illegal?

The time to decide how to handle a crisis is NOW, before it happens. Anticipate every situation you can imagine and have a plan ready. That's the difference between being an employee and being in charge. You are the planner, you are the one who copes.

ON THE PHONE

There are many areas to consider here. I'll start from the minute a customer calls to inquire about your work, your prices, deadlines, etc., and I'll go through all the processes. I think the easiest way to illustrate my points so that you understand what I mean is for me to give you guidelines based on my experience, and sprinkle in conversation examples.

First decide how you will answer your telephone.
On page 102 we talked about this a little bit. First
you smile and are cheerful. Then you figure out what
to say. It can be as simple as "hello," or as complicated as "Good afternoon, Sandy's Secretarial Service.
How may I help you?"

In my academic business, I preferred "hello." I
didn't have a separate phone line for my business, and
I never knew if a caller was for my business or for one
of the kids or for my husband. I felt it was presump-
tious of me to answer the only phone in the house by
saying, "Hello, Peggy Glenn, professional typist."

However, if you have a separate line installed in
your home, and if you operate with a fictitious business name, then by all means answer that telephone line
with your company name. As already discussed on page
90, when deciding on a company name, consider how easy
it will be to say when answering the phone. A real
tongue-twister can be embarrassing, and may be a
drawback.

I think there is an advantage to this set-up if
you will be typing for businesses; that is, if you
specialize in business typing. Somehow you'll have
more identification and credibility in the business
world if you are "Pat's Secretarial Service" or
"Terri's Typing" than if you are just another "hello"
on the end of the line. There again, and I know you're
probably tired of reading it by now but it's the truth,
YOU know your customers. You know yourself. Don't
take my word as THE word. Use that mind of your own.

Once you've figured out how to answer the phone,
always be sure that you get a customer's name and
telephone number as soon as you have any formal contact. If you don't catch the name the first time, ask
again in the middle of the conversation. People enjoy
being addressed by name. The difference between anony-
mity and reality is their name. When the call is completed, address her or him by name and say, "Thank you,
Ann, I'll be looking forward to our 3 o'clock appointment."

Why the number? If you have set up an appointment, for example, you may need to be able to get in
touch with him or her if you have an emergency and must
reschedule the appointment. In addition, once you have
the customer's work, having the phone number will
enable you to call to check on any discrepancies (words

left out, words you can't read, something that doesn't make sense, etc.).

After you have finished typing for that customer, jot his or her number on a 3 x 5 file card and keep it handy. In the beginning it is nice to call customers every few months and remind them that you enjoyed typing for them and are available if they need more work done. You can also thank them for any referrals they have sent. That's an extension of both the advertising and publicity lessons from the previous chapters.

If they have mentioned a possible deadline, and you haven't received the work yet, reminding them that it is approaching may be just the memory-jog they need to get working on the paper and get you to type it.

As an another example of good P.R. (public relations) and good record-keeping, suppose that Customer "A" is a computer expert, and Customer "B" just happens to need someone to write a program for his bill collecting. Offer to put the two of them together. Maintain confidentiality while arranging this meeting, however. You mention to Customer B that you have a possible solution for his problem because you know of Customer A. You "know of" customer A, you don't work for him. Carry through that way, and if both parties agree to be contacted, then give away both phone numbers.

As another example, if Customer "Y" makes hand-painted beer mugs and you need one for a gift, you'll have your own personal Yellow Pages.

BEFORE

NEVER, NEVER, NEVER commit yourself to a price quote or a time quote on the telephone without first seeing the work. You can quote your hourly or per/page prices, but don't quote a finished price or a definite deadline.

One of the most uncomfortable experiences I had was when I'd been in business for about 2 weeks. A man called at 10 a.m. and said he had ten pages of typing that he needed for a meeting the next morning. Because my specialty is academic typing, I assumed he meant double-spaced typing. For some stupid reason I also assumed I'd be typing from handwritten or rough-typed copy.

As it turned out, he was a real estate salesman who had seen my ad on a college bulletin board. He assumed I was a student and that he could get cheap labor and demand a lot.

When he arrived, the ten pages were to be done single-spaced in elite type with only a 3/4 inch margin on the left, and half an inch on the top, right, and bottom. That's approximately four times as much work as is on a page of double-spaced pica typing with standard academic margins.

The copy I was to type from was also single-spaced with numerous scratch-outs, write-overs, and inserts on separate slips of paper that were attached in no particular order. I had to hunt for each insert among the miscellaneous scraps.

To make matters worse, I had told him on the phone that the job would cost him about $10 or $12 and that I could get it done by early evening. (That was when I first started and I gave almost every customer same-day or next-day service.)

The clock chimed noon, and I swallowed hard at having been so naive. I almost pushed him out the door so I could get started right away. I knew the afternoon was going to be too short for what I had to do.

He couldn't have driven five blocks when he stopped at a pay phone and called me with a correction that he had forgotten. During the rest of the afternoon he called me six more times with corrections -- two of them were corrections to the corrections. I had to type four pages over, and by 5 o'clock I was a wreck!

I finally took the phone off the hook so that I could finish the job. He was supposed to pick it up at 6:30. He showed up at 7:15 and was very angry that the phone had been busy and that he hadn't been able to give me two more corrections!

I mumbled something about teenagers on the phone and numbly took the $10 he shoved at me. I knew good and well that the job was worth at least $40, and at that time I couldn't afford to be duped out of $30. Right then and there I made up my mind that I'd never type for him again. I also promised myself never to commit myself on the phone for a deadline or finished price. BUT, I held my cool. I thanked him for his

business, and gave him my card. The old "service with
a smile and clenched teeth" routine.

    Believe it or not, he called me about two weeks
later and asked if I were free to do some more work for
him. We were having tuna sandwiches for supper and the
menu for the rest of the week was dismal, but I decided
that HE wasn't worth it!

    Here's the line I gave him.

        "Oh, Mr. Johnson, now nice to hear
    from you. I'm so sorry! I just this
    morning took on a job that will keep me
    booked through next Wednesday. I wish I
    could type for you. Can I help you find
    another typist? I'm sure if you call the
    colleges or secretarial services in the
    Yellow Pages you can find someone to help
    you right away. I know your work is
    important and demands immediate atten-
    tion."

    Now, I ask you! Is that a line? And I delivered
it without busting out in laughter or being struck by
lightning for lying through my teeth. I wasn't sicky
sweet, either. But he thinks I was really impressed by
his C-R-A-P. I'll tell you what, though -- over the

next 2 years I never typed for him again, but he sent me over $400 worth of business via referrals from folks he knew. He told them all how gracious I was, how I went out of my way to help him when I couldn't do his work.

Mind you, when I referred him to another service, I chose one that operated in an office and charged more because of their overhead. Then I alerted the other service and they dealt with him before he could cause them any grief. In truth, they were better equipped to handle his needs. There were three typists and a manager who could put the "power" on one of his jobs if he needed it. He also had to schedule appointments, and they made sure he paid a premium if he was late bringing in the work. His work was "business" and I enjoyed "academic." We were all happy. That's that networking and referral I talked about in the very first chapter. There's more about it later.

*　　*　　*　　*

Since then I've never been badgered into a phone quote for prices or deadlines. Here's a typical initial phone conversation with a customer. My "lines" are in the bold type, the "customer" talks in regular type.

"Hello, I'm calling about typing. Is this Peggy Glenn?"

"Yes, speaking. How can I help you?"

"Well, I have a little term paper that I need to have typed. Can you do it and how much will it cost me?"

"First I need to know how long it is, what shape it's in right now, and when you need it."

"We-e-e-l-l-l-l, the teacher said it was supposed to be about 14 pages, I'm not finished writing it, and it's due Friday."

"That may be a problem; this is Wednesday. Does the paper have footnotes or tables? Do you need help with spelling, grammar, or punctuation?"

"Yeah, it'll need a little fixing up. And the teacher said it was up to us if we used footnotes; but it has to have a bibliography. Do you know what that is? What I really need to know, though, is how much it's gonna cost me."

"My rates are $10 an hour or a minimum of $1.50 per double-spaced page depending on what I'm typing from and what the finished product will be. I type 90 words-a-minute, but if I can't read it, or if it is technical material, I can't go that fast."

"Oh." (long pause) "Well, do you think I can get out of it for less than $15?"

"That'll depend entirely on how well I can read what you give me, if you get it here in time for me to do it, how many pages it ends up being, and how much I have to fix it up."

"You mean you can't tell me for sure that it won't cost me more than $15?"

"That's right! I can't be sure until I see your work. I don't want to mislead you and then surprise you when you come to pick up the work. I'll be happy to give you an estimate before I type it, but I can't tell you anything more until I actually see the work."

"O.K. Well, I'll finish it up this afternoon and bring it to you in the morning. Is that okay?"

"Yes, the morning will be all right, but I _have_ to have it by 10 o'clock if I'm expected to give it back to you for a Friday morning class. I need the whole day to type it, and I want to proofread it again Friday morning before you pick it up. This time there will be no RUSH charge, but in the future, if I have less than 2 days, I charge time-and-a-half. It's for your own protection. If I have to rush on a job, I run the risk of making errors, and that's not fair to you. That's not what you pay for. I hope you understand."

Always make _them_ responsible for the decisions. Try to let them know that you have _their_ best interest at heart. You don't want your customers to think that you are a mercenary who lays in wait for poor innocents. You want them to think that their work is _THE_ most important piece You will handle that day. That they really count with you!

You can't always size up the customers on the phone. Sometimes the most polished and sincere-sounding customer on the phone turns out to be a real ogre

```
                        STATEMENT


                      PEGGY GLENN
                  PROFESSIONAL TYPIST


    ┌ .
          #1 Crabby Customer

          School of Unpleasantness


    └

    XXXXXXXXXXXXXXXXXXXXXXXXXXXXXXXXXXXXXXXXXXXXXXXXXXXXX RECEIPT.
```

1/7	Consultation regarding typing 1 hour	$7.00
1/8	Typing--12 pages @ $1.25	15.00
	6 phone calls @ 15 min/each (90 min @ $7/hr)	10.50
	Call to library to check incomplete reference--30 min.	3.50
1/9	Corrections to 8 pages to correct customer's error (retyping necessary)	10.00
1/9	Additional phone calls--30 min.	3.50
		$49.50

Thank you for your business. Be sure to recommend me
to your friends who need accurate and thorough work by
a PROFESSIONAL.   Peggy Glenn

                                    PAID BY CHECK NO.

8K 884 Rediform

once you are working on the paper, or when he or she comes to pick up the work.

In my business, the majority of the difficult customers were male. I think it's because they were so used to categorizing women as subservient. In spite of my best efforts, to some of them I was still "just a secretary." They didn't view me as an equal -- as a professional -- until they received my bill. In all fairness to the male of the species, however, nearly all my customers were pleasant. My point here is that of the few who were difficult, the majority of them were male.

In my experience, women have been more tolerant and more accepting of me as an equal partner in the production of a quality typewritten document. They are the writers, and I am the polisher. It's kind of like the collaboration of cookbook author and experienced cook who can work as a team, or design artist and production engineer.

DURING

DON'T PUT UP WITH rudeness, disrespect, or needless interruptions. Make them pay for their ill manners or arrogance.

I once knew a traffic officer who said that the more belligerent a person became, the more he "stuck it to 'em" with his pencil and citation book. The same principle can be applied in the home-based typing business. The more arrogant a customer is -- the more he or she interrupts you, or the more you have to go out of your way to fix up the work you're doing without any appreciation from them -- the more times you hit the "add" key on the calculator.

An itemized invoice or bill is the best way to persuade this kind of customer that you are above that sort of treatment. I've included one here for you to see exactly what I mean.

Sometimes when I get an over-anxious customer who just seems to have a case of the jitters and isn't sure you're going to be finished with his or her work, I simply avoid answering the phone. I turn on my answering device and put a message on it that says something like:

Thank you for calling. Right now I'm
tied up with a very important typing project for a special customer. I must pay
close attention to what I'm doing to
avoid errors. I appreciate your understanding. At the sound of the tone,
please leave your name and number, and
I'll call back as soon as possible.

That is usually enough to humble the most arrogant
customer, and ease the fears of the ones who worry too
much. At the same time, I can monitor the incoming
calls. If I hear a message that I must answer, I simply cut in on the machine. My family is used to it,
too. Their standard message is, "Mom, are you there?"
If I am really not at home, they usually leave a message. It's become a joke around here: "Mom, are you
there?"

*   *   *   *

ALWAYS PROOFREAD your work one more time before
the customer arrives.

I always allowed myself one extra day on the deadline just for proofreading. I usually put the work
away for the night and proofread it first thing the
next morning when my brain was fresh. Many times I
picked up a small error that could be fixed in no time
at all, but which would probably would have irritated
the customer, especially if the work were being turned
in to an important class. Whether it's academic,
medical, legal, business, or for writers, it's supposed
to be correct.

(I hope there aren't any errors in this book.
It's been proofread by at least 4 people, and not all
of them caught all the same errors. If you find one,
please just forgive me and them. We did our very best.
Please don't write me letters about them. You know
I'll find them myself the week after this comes from
the printer, and I'll be embarrassed enough already.)

Here's one of the easiest methods: use a ruler
and a soft pencil. Read the work aloud to be sure
there are no words left out. By having to say the
words, there is a better chance of catching errors.
When you find a mistake, mark a small "x" lightly in
the margin opposite the line that contains the error.
By not marking in the text, you eliminate having to
retype the whole page.

So what happens if you've proofread, found no errors, and one shows up later (either you missed it or the customer's copy was wrong to start with). My standard policy for "who pays for mistakes" was: If the error was mine (word or phrase left out, words repeated, typographical errors, pages numbered wrong, etc.), I redid the work or repaired the mistakes at absolutely no charge to the customer.

However, if the customer had left out a vital part of the work, or the handwriting was illegible, I charged for redoing any pages necessary. This is only fair.

Sometimes when you're extremely busy, or when you've typed more than one draft of a paper, you might want to hire someone else to do the proofreading. I had very good luck with a retired schoolteacher. She was overjoyed to be needed, she enjoyed reading college or university papers, and she paid close attention to every detail. She picked up such small things as duplicate page numbers, missing page numbers, and dates that didn't correspond in separate sections of a thesis. She also caught it when I forgot to close a quotation.

She charged me only about 7¢ a page to have her take the responsibility for proofreading, and my customers really appreciated the added time and effort I took with their work. It's another of those small extras that can make a home-based typing business look so professional!

* * * *

ALWAYS MEET YOUR DEADLINES if humanly possible. If there is the slightest possibility that you will be unable to meet a customer's deadline, call the customer immediately and explain your circumstances. The sooner you let the customer know, the more likely it is that you'll be forgiven...and the sooner the customer can make her or his own arrangements for the delay.

I had to back out just once. I called the woman about 3 days in advance to tell her that I was sick with the flu and wasn't positive that I could meet her deadline. I offered to find another typist to help me, I offered to call her instructor, and I offered to give her the completed part of the paper to prove to the instructor that the delay was my fault and not hers. You know how often a professor hears, "My typist didn't finish it yet."

My customer was absolutely great to me in return! She said that I didn't need to worry, that she would call her instructor right away and explain the circumstances and that if her instructor had a problem, she (the customer) would take it up with the dean. This was her last paper of the semester and all of her other papers had been turned in on time.

I didn't expect that kind of response from my customer, but it was clear she was in my corner. She quickly reassured me and then told me to get lots of rest, take two aspirin, and call her when I was done with her paper. Familiar advice with an unfamiliar refrain.

That kind of rapport is necessary with customers, especially repeaters. You can establish that rapport by being honest and reliable with your customers from the beginning. I value that sort of relationship almost more than I value the money. That is the kind of mutual respect that I never had in a job. But I have it now in my business and it is very, very nice. That's another one of the many ways in which I measure my "success."

*   *   *   *

PAY ATTENTION TO SMALL DETAILS. Whenever you can improve on a customer's work by correcting spelling, rearranging awkward sentences, fixing punctuation, etc., do it. If you catch an error in addition, or any mathematical equation, check with the customer and then put in the correct number(s).

This thoroughness and personalized touch will make you a valuable asset to your customers. This is one of the reasons they will be willing to pay you well. Being conscientious and careful isn't quite enough, though. You also have to tell them about it. Point out where you put forth extra effort, where you fixed errors, where you improved. They need to know it.

If you haven't been able to justify a high price in the beginning, as soon as you get a supply of steady customers, you can raise your prices gradually and they'll never ever complain. If they do, they probably aren't worth your talents. That may sound crude and egotistical, but if you think highly of yourself, so will your customers. If you don't, they won't, and you'll never receive the respect you deserve nor be paid the price you deserve.

One other feature I have for regular customers is the "absent drop-off and pick-up." If I'm not home, they are free to put their work through a slot in my front door. If I must leave the house before they are able to pick up their work, I sometimes enclose the finished work in an envelope that I attach to the front door. They simply pick up their work and leave my money or check in the mail slot which drops directly into the house.

I do this ONLY with regular customers. I don't want strangers slipping things through my door slot, and I don't want to broadcast about when I'll be away from home. When setting up appointments I sometimes tell little white lies to guarantee my free time.

> I'm sorry, but I can't see you until
> 6:30 p.m. I have customers in the morn-
> ing and afternoon, and would prefer to
> schedule you for an appointment after
> I've finished eating my dinner.

What I didn't say was that I was going shopping with a friend in the morning, and had an appointment with the orthodontist in the afternoon. I had already made those plans, but didn't want to advertise that no one would be home. Nor did I want to cancel my shopping trip. Every- one deserves a little break now and then. (I also turn on the answering machine so people think I'm hard at work.) Ah-h-h, the luxuries of self- employment and self-regulation of one's schedule.

AFTER

DON'T TAKE CHECKS from a customer on the first visit (unless that customer is a business or you feel the customer would be grossly offended, and why would an honest customer take offense).

Again, I got burned once. My now-standard pitch is:

> I prefer not to take checks until I
> have established a business relationship
> with you. I had one unpleasant experi-
> ence trying to collect on a bad check,
> and I'd rather not have an adversary

association with you. I'd be happy to
give you a receipt for tax purposes, but
until I have typed for you on a more
regular basis, I'm sure you can honor my
policy of cash.

That speech works like a charm. No one has
refused to pay me, and no one has been uncomfortable
about paying me in cash. Of course, I tell them this
when they _first_ leave the work with me; sometimes I
tell them on the telephone before the appointment in
case the job is large and I would need to require a
deposit. It would be pretty embarrassing to have to
make a customer come back another time.

Now, obviously, if you type for well-established
businesses or professional people, you can't always
follow that rule. Occasionally you must be flexible.
But it is imperative that you stick to it when dealing
with individuals. There is no guarantee that you will
see them again. And once they have the finished
typed product, what's to stop them from
disappearing from your life forever?
Cash-and-carry -- it's been the way in
our country since the days of the
Pilgrims.

By the same token, don't give back
the work if the customer shows up without
cash or checkbook. In this case I don't
mind asking the customer to make a second
trip. They understood right from the
start what my policy was regarding payment.
The only time I make allowances is when I've been
typing for a customer on a regular basis for several
months. Then occasionally I've been known to "slide"
them until payday if they forgot or were "short."

*   *   *   *

KEEP IN TOUCH with the pleasant customers. As I
mentioned on the second page of this chapter, a good
rapport between you and your customers is an invaluable
business asset.

Keep a 3 x 5 card file (or an address book) with
all your customers' names, phone numbers, and
addresses. You never know when you might need to contact one of them. If you deal with business or professional customers, you might consider sending them holiday greeting cards in November or December.

As I mentioned earlier, don't hesitate to contact a customer if you feel you can offer assistance in his or her subject area (or if you need information that one of them might have). This is how the "good old boy" networks get started.

You can develop a reliable resource list in a short time. After only about a year, my pile of 3 x 5 cards had outgrown the rubber band and graduated to one of those plastic boxes with A-Z dividers. Occasionally I review the file to update addresses and phone numbers. I rarely throw out a card, but I have been known to part with some if I didn't hear from the customer for over a year. This will be up to you.

ETHICS

Confidentiality, how much "editing" is fair for college students," what to do when asked to plagiarize, what to do when asked to alter a document, what to do when asked to do a "little investigative letter-writing and phone calling." You don't think it'll happen? It may not, but then again it may. Give some thought to these issues now and be prepared to stand your ground without compromise. Each of you will deal with these issues differently.

CONFIDENTIALITY. Consider this scenario:

> A customer brings you a resume, and that customer is obviously already employed in one position but is seeking employment somewhere else. She leaves you a telephone number. You finish the resume early and call her up. She's not at her desk, so you leave the following message with a clerk: "This is ABC Secretarial. Please tell Joanie that her new resume is finished."

Whoa! Now at least one person at her present job knows that Joanie is having her resume redone; whether she wants them to know is another story. They don't know if she's trying for an internal promotion or if Joanie is looking around for a new position. You've seriously compromised your confidentiality with customer, Joanie. But be open about it. If you've made such a serious error, try to reach her again to tell her about it immediately so that she can cover her tracks -- if it isn't too late.

Here's another example. Suppose one of your clients is a private investigator or a psychologist or an investigative reporter who is working on a "hot book"? In any of these instances, and in many more, you'll be typing or transcribing material which must be kept in the strictest confidence. Acknowledge and accept this responsibility, and you'll always have plenty of work. Betray this confidentiality, and your business is doomed.

EDITING FOR COLLEGE STUDENTS.

When do you draw the line? When is it cheating for you to rewrite a customer's work, particularly a student? When is it acceptable? Here's how I handled it. If my thinking helps you form your policy, I'm pleased. This is a difficult one for many folks, and I hope I can help you through it.

The bulk of my typing business was academic, and the majority of that work was performing minor and/or major editing for my clients. Depending on the client, I applied one of several standards. For a beginning freshman student, I would not perform anything but very minor spelling, punctuation, and verb/subject agreement editing. I figured that someone fresh from high school (and I talk here of the young freshman rather than someone returning to school after years of working) would only continue to be deluded about his/her lack of skills if someone like me fixed it up time and time again before it was turned into the instructor.

I also found out, much to my complete dismay, that many of the teachers didn't know what was correct, and beyond that, that they didn't care if the student per-formed well grammatically as long as a paper came in and as long as the paper presented good ideas in a logical format.

On the other hand, a lot of my clients were people who had been working for as many as 20 years at a vocation, i.e., nurses, firemen, policemen. In many cases, training for these jobs 15-20 years ago was not academic, but rather vocational. And some of them had received no formal college schooling at all, only on-the-job training.

In order to advance (and sometimes to stay afloat) in their field, these people now needed to obtain at least a bachelor's degree, and some tried desperately

for a master's degree. Often they were still working
full time while attending accelerated-pace programs at
off-site campus locations. In addition to this brutal
schedule, many of them were handicapped further. Most
of these clients were locked into the jargon of their
professions; most of them didn't know correct written
sentence structure. Their vocabulary was pitifully
shallow.

They were paying me as a consultant, as a trans-
lator -- I changed their words from jargon into
academese. I was proud and not offended to provide
extensive editing and in some cases rewriting for these
clients. I rationalized that businesses employ professional writers and editors for this very function. I
saw my work as an extension of my clients' business
efforts, rather than as an attempt to subvert the
educational process.

In between the 19-year-old freshman and the 45-
year-old freshman were all kinds of other clients. I
used a variety of editing skills to meet their needs
and still satisfy my conscience.

PLAGIARIZE.

I couldn't. First, I'm a writer by profession,
was a writer then, when I was typing. I couldn't. For
me it was personal, and not a matter of professional
ethics. Second, I'd been a student and worked hard for
my grades, struggled with research, written rough
drafts and edited drafts. Third, I'd been a secretary
to college and university professors, and I didn't like
the idea of some student passing a fast one on a professor. Here again, running your own business allows
you to make decisions and justify them. Refusing to
accept work from a client is a lot different from
refusing to do work for a supervisor. In the first
instance, it's okay. In the second, you'd be fired.

However, I've talked with dozens of other typists
whose policy is, "We'll type anything. It's not our
position to judge." I don't argue with their decision.
I don't think they're wrong. I couldn't do it, but
that doesn't make it wrong. Decide in your own mind
how you feel about this issue and have your speech prepared (or none if you don't need one) when the first
college student brings a paper to you that he or she is
copying from the library or has purchased from a term-
paper broker.

ALTERING A LEGAL OR IMPORTANT DOCUMENT.

For many of the same emotional and philosophical
reasons, I refused this kind of work, also. I'm not
sure if I could have been held criminally liable (an
attorney might have had to prove that I was aware of
what I was doing if I had done it), but I didn't want
to take the chance and I couldn't morally or ethically
do it. I almost was assaulted over that one. I guess
my "No" speech was a little defensive or a little
preachy. If it hadn't been for my dog and my screen
door, I'd have been in trouble, I think.

INVESTIGATING, SNOOPING.

I felt that if a customer wanted me to make telephone inquiries or send letters of inquiry, then that
customer should be willing to pay me the going rate for
a private investigator. However, I didn't have the
courage to come right out and say this, so I simply
said I was too busy.

WHAT ELSE COULD GO WRONG?

You could be asked to type letters that you know
contain lies. For example, a worker's compensation
appeal letter from a man who claims an incapacitating
back injury, but who drops off the work while on his
way to participate in a bowling tournament. For
another example, a woman who is receiving generous
financial support from "a friend" while applying for a
college loan to the disadvantaged.

A foreign student who can barely read your ad
brings you a paper that is obviously written by someone
else. Will you type it?

But this was the kicker for me? How would you
have reacted?

        I had been typing for Mr. X for almost
     2 years. He was attending college nights
     in addition to his regular job. Either
     Mr. X or his messenger would deliver and
     pick up the work. Within weeks after his
     graduation, I received a call from a
     woman who identified herself as Mrs. X.
     It seems that Mr. X and his messenger
     were "very close friends," and now Mrs. X

wanted to know the name, address, phone
number, and vital statistics on the messenger. I didn't know, and hadn't paid
attention since she had always been identified as "the messenger" and I naively
thought that was her only function. I
knew nothing and was, for once, grateful
for my ignorance.

If I had known, if I had been privy to the situation, how should I have handled the telephone call from
Mrs. X? I realize that hindsight is always much
sharper than foresight, but I think I'd have played
ignorant even if I hadn't been. Why? Mainly because
I'm too selfish to have allowed my valuable typing time
(MONEY-MAKING time, remember) to be caught up in a
court case. Secondarily, my business was typing, and I
preferred to keep all client contacts confidential.

You'll have a "kicker," too. Suppose a presiden-
tial advisor showed up at your door with a confidential
memo. When they travel, who do you suppose does their
typing? Suppose, suppose, suppose -- anything's
possible. Be confidential, be professional, and be
paid well.

SUMMARY

I don't know where I got my glib tongue or where I
came up with all those snazzy-sounding things to say.
My father says it's Irish malarkey, and my husband has
another word for it (expletive deleted). I call it
customer management with a little of the feminine survival instinct thrown in for good measure. You call it
whatever you choose -- as long as it works for you.

If you hold your temper, conduct yourself as a professional businesswoman, plan ahead for all sorts of
unusual or out of the ordinary occurrences, and stick
to the few basic guidelines I've presented here, you'll
be happy and successful.

When I make my customers feel important (even when
they are obnoxious or insignificant), when I make them
see me as a real pro (even if I'm maybe still an
amateur), when they know I'll respect their need for
privacy and confidentiality, and when I get them off my
back so I can enjoy my business -- then I've accom-
plished what I set out to do. I'm running my business;
it's not running me.

149

Few people do business well who do nothing else.

— LORD CHESTERFIELD, 1749

10
TAKING CARE

The biggest investment in your home-based typing business is YOU. You are far more valuable than any piece of equipment you can buy, rent, lease, or borrow. Without YOU, none of that equipment can operate.

Imagine that your body is the latest in automotive technology -- one of a kind -- only highly-trained and highly-paid specialists can work on it. You can't afford to have that body break down, and your budget can't afford any repair bills. Unplanned "down-time" is minus-revenue; and replacement parts (bionics, transplants) are still in the experimental stage (which is scientific talk for very expensive!).

Just as every school teacher has told you, and just as you hear on TV and read in the best women's magazines, diet, exercise, rest, and fun are very, very important. What you put into your body and how you keep it in shape will determine what kind of job it will do for you when you need it the most.

Now, I'm not advocating that you stock up on health foods, become a vegetarian, or abstain from alcohol or tobacco. That's not what I mean at all. What I am saying is that you should eat ONLY what you need, eat a balanced diet (as best as inflation will let you), get exercise other than pounding the type-writer keyboard, get plenty of rest, and plan recreation and fun. These few basic common-sense guidelines will truly make a difference in how trouble-free your self-employment will be.

How can I be so sure? How can I preach to you this way? I've made the mistake of too little exercise

and too little rest and too little fun. The mistake
cost me time away from work, cost me money for medical
bills, and caused significant disruption in my personal
life. Would you ever think it was possible to hate the
sight and sound of a typewriter? Pound on it for 12 or
14 hours a day, for too many days in a row, and see?
You'll hate it and so will everyone around you.

DENNIS the MENACE

"I DIDN'T MEAN TO EAT IT ALL UP...BUT THE PART THAT
WAS LEFT KEPT GETTIN' SMALLER AN' SMALLER, TILL IT WAS
HARDLY WORTH SAVIN'."

DIET

You have all learned about the basic 4 food
groups. Meat, Dairy, Cereal, and Vegetable/Fruit.
That's grade school stuff. What you might also do is
look through your favorite cookbook and take note of
the foods you normally eat which are highest in calories. Eliminate some of them from your diet because
you won't need as many calories once you sit in the
typing chair for more than a week.

Substitute those high-calorie munchies for some with fewer calories and maybe more food value. After 3 years I can finally pass up salted cashews for a juicy, ice-cold apple, but I still have trouble eating celery in place of Oreos and a nice cold glass of milk.

Maybe my strategy will work for you. The one sure way for me to eat less is simply to buy and cook less. If the food doesn't appear on the table, I can't eat it. I hate putting away the leftovers, and I also hate to throw things away, so I always used to eat them instead. The large economy size food doesn't really save me money if I have to buy new large economy-size clothes.

If you've been working at an outside job before starting your typing business, you will probably start to put on weight right through the sitting part of your once-beautiful body. There is a strong tendency for home-based typists to walk less and less because now even the walk from the bus stop, subway station, or parking lot has been eliminated. With a home-based business, you walk only from room to room.

Consequently, muscles get soft, and the calories taken in are more than those expended. The dial or numbers on the scales go up as does the size of the clothes in your wardrobe, and also the potential for health problems. I'm no one to talk, I've made the mistakes. And I'm trying to undo them still.

If you haven't been used to working outside the home, and you start a busines on top of your household job, you may find much the same problem. Typing doesn't expend the same energy that pushing a vacuum does, and you will probably push the vacuum less frequently anyway once you start your business. So, you simply require less to eat UNLESS you do something else to use up those unexpended calories. Read later on in the exercise and fun sections.

Suppose you intend to use your typing business as extra income -- that is, in addition to a "real job" in the "real world." In this instance, you may face the problem of eating poorly because you will be pushed for time and will grab for junk foods and convenience foods in an effort to have more time to type. All I can say is, please, use caution. Keep a mental note of what you are eating. When you start to feel plump around the edges or sluggish and irritable, look to your diet as a possible part of the reason.

EXERCISE

All of that stuff I just said about watching your food applies equally to watching your exercise level. Weight-gain is a significant and very obvious result of too little exercise. In addition, lack of exercise and toning can mean that you'll push your body beyond its limits. This phenomenon sneaks up on you, though. And curing the problem takes almost as long as getting the problem. That time will cost you money.

The muscles of the upper and lower back, neck, and arms must be conditioned and kept in shape if they are to give you the best service. Muscles which are not kept in shape become fatigued and subject to injury.

Typing is an almost constant isometric exercise. Too much of it is disastrous. If you're a little skeptical, or if you believe me but don't know exactly what I mean, do this:

Sit in a chair or stand up. Place your elbows even with your waistline, and not quite touching your body. Bend your arm 90° at the elbow, so that your forearm is parallel to the floor. Now, wiggle your fingers for 10 minutes. Feel the strain? Wiggle them for another 10 minutes. Don't move your elbows, don't move your wrists, don't move your shoulders. Simply hold your arms still and wiggle your fingers.

Yes, now maybe you can see how hours and hours of this a day with no break, with no conditioning, can set you up for pain, discomfort, and very real injury. To avoid the intrusion of this pain and injury, do something else with your body to keep it in shape and to relieve the tension of constant typing (the mental tension as well as the muscle tension).

I'm not saying that you have to lift weights or train as much as an athlete does; but you must do something to keep in shape, and you should do it every day. Check with your doctor before you start, so that you don't exceed your cardiac or respiratory limits. Also check with an exercise specialist for what's best for you. Explain how you use your arms. He or she will be able to develop a set of very simple exercises that will keep you in shape to do the job. Once you start on a program, stick to it. Make as much of a commitment to your health as you do to your business.

What can you do for exercise? There are a lot of alternatives. Probably the least expensive (and least embarrassing if you tend to shy away from parading your body in a leotard) is to tune in the television set to a show that calls for at-home participation in a carefully planned exercise program. As far as I can find out, nearly every area of the country has at least one such show in its daily repertoire. As I write this, Richard Simmons is the current rage.

Another nearly free alternative is a daily walk. Perhaps you can walk to the bank each day with the money you made the previous day. Walking has mental health benefits as well as fitness benefits. Half an hour's walk in the fresh air is supposed to be good for clearing the mind and relieving tension. That's what all the experts in the magazines say, anyway.

I love my walk. It's nearly the only time of the day I can call my own. There are no phone interruptions and I feel like a new person when I come home after half an hour. I always take a different route, and I bet I can tell you every home within 5 miles of me that has a barking dog, needs a roof repaired, could use a coat of paint. You'd also be surprised how many decorating and landscaping ideas I wish I had time and money to implement. Oh, well, one of these days. Daydreaming is fun.

I also ride my bike when I have to travel any distance or have light shopping to do. I use my bicycle when I'm especially tired or have been working unusually hard on a project. I seem to unwind more on my bike than I do on foot.

Tennis, running, swimming, skiing, rollerskating, and dancing are popular in different parts of the country. These activities also burn up lots of calories as well as providing good exercise. The latest booklet from the President's Council on Physical Fitness has a complete list of calories expended in these activities.

To get a copy of this booklet, send 60¢, your name and address, and specify booket 121H to:

Consumer Information Center
Pueblo, Colorado 81009

If you have the money and the time, you can join a health club, exercise spa, or even sign up for a bowling league. Whatever you like to do best, DO IT. No cheating, though, you're the only one who will suffer.

Those of you with young children may want to use your exercise time to satisfy the demand for mother's time. Take your infant or young child to the park, for a walk around the block, or do some other activity that makes you happy and gives you some exercise at the same time. Parents are particularly creative at "double-timing," doing two things at once without making it look as if that's what you've done.

Older children can be engaged in a game of hop-scotch, jumprope, hide and seek, tag, etc. The list and possibilities are endless. Use your imagination, look at yourself and your family, and then just do something.

If you don't have children, but would like to do something with a child -- borrow one. I'm sure you can talk a neighbor into giving up a child for an hour or two. I know I would have done it gladly when my kids were younger -- I might still do it now that they're teenagers. Maybe you can strike up a deal. You take their youngster off their hands for an hour or two, and they'll answer your business phone so you don't miss any chances to make more money.

TAKE BREAKS

In addition to planned exercise, take a break from the typewriter -- at least 10 minutes out of every hour. Stand up from the chair, take some deep breaths, walk around, do a few neck rolls, wave your arms as if you were trying to kill a swarm of moths, do some stretching exercises, and maybe do a couple of jumping jacks.

This not only relaxes the arms, shoulders, and neck, it

clears the brain. One wise old doctor whom I know says that physical activity gets the blood flowing faster. This in turn pumps more blood to the brain which is why, he says, I can think better after one of these homemade exercise routines. I'll take his word for it.

I don't know if his theory is entirely accurate, but I do know I feel better when I do it. Even when I'm facing a deadline, I stick to this 50 minutes of typing / 10 minutes of flapping-in-the-breeze routine. I make fewer mistakes and get the job done with less wear and tear on my one-of-a-kind human machine.

This same 50/10 schedule, or any modification of it that suits you best, should be followed even if you are physically disabled, if you're medically retired, or restricted in your physical activity in any other way. As soon as you start to feel tired and or your muscles feel tight while typing, TAKE A BREAK.

Stop until the tension goes away. If you're in a wheelchair, for instance, push the chair away from the typewriter, move to another room, look out the window, have a snack (low-calories, now), and try some mental relaxation techniques. When you've got the cobwebs pushed aside, it's time to hit the keys again.

REST UP

There have been lots of articles written on how some people need more or less sleep than others. I read them all, I believe them all, and then I get what MY body and mind seem to ask for. Some nights I get along well on 6 hours; other nights I need 8, 9, or 10 hours of sleep. And sometimes when I take my 10-minute break for relaxation, I find myself taking a short cat-nap.

That's okay! That's why I'm in business for myself. That's one of the things you will enjoy, too. If you need a day off, if you need a few hours for yourself, if you need to sleep-in and be lazy for half a day -- do it. The only one you must answer to or justify this schedule to is YOU. Just be sure you can meet your deadlines.

Allow yourself time to rest. A normal eight-hour day's output is between 35 and 50 pages of double-spaced typing when working from hand-written copy. Normal from transcription may be higher (if you can understand it). Normal output for letters, financial documents, or technical documents will differ. It all depends on what you are capable of doing and how well you can read the customer's work. Don't commit yourself to producing more than you can handle. Schedule breaks and rest periods and even occasional days off. You will need it.

Don't be a worse boss than the one you just had.

HAVE SOME FUN

All work and no play makes the home-based typist:

_____

fill in your own worst idea

After you have eaten right, done enough exercise, taken sufficient breaks, and had adequate rest, try to squeeze in some FUN. That can range from a week in Tahiti to a few hours of gardening and everything in between such as: having lunch with a friend, going to a movie, going camping, window shopping, etc.

On the average of once a week, take time out for YOU. This should be time that is completely separate from family time. If you are single, it should be fairly easy. If you are not single, it may be a little more difficult. But maybe just soaking in the tub for half an hour with the door closed is your idea of luxury and something special. With a little luck and some careful planning you can find time and money for treats -- real ones and mental ones.

Even if your business is barely managing to provide you with a survival income, plan to at least take
some time, just a few hours will do -- invent something
fun. You know what your interests are, and you know
what will give you pleasure. Do it. You worked hard,
you earned it. Maybe while you're out having some fun
you'll be struck with a fantastic idea to find new
clients.

SUMMARY

    In summary, eat well but only what you need; keep
your body in shape so it can do the very best for you
when you depend on it to be there; get enough rest so
that you are sharp and alert to do the kind of job your
customer is paying for; and enjoy yourself. Be good to
your body and mind, and they'll return the favor.

    If you do all of that, the maintenance contract on
your most expensive (and least expendable) piece of
equipment will be renewed by the manufacturer from year
to year.

                    *   *   *   *

Another Peggy P.S.:
    You might wonder why this chapter is in a book
about how to run a business. The information isn't
new, we've all heard it before. BUT, once we become
self-employed, our personal health takes on greater
significance. Our "sick days" cost us money. I'm not
talking here in this chapter about real illnesses,
unavoidable accidents, or unplanned misfortunes. No
one can predict when those will enter our daily
calendar. Rather, this is a prevention chapter to
avoid setting ourselves up for trouble and/or failure.
I really felt that if I were going to help you prepare
yourself to be in business, I ought to tell you all the
story that I know, not just the good parts. As obvious
as the need for good health is, we often overlook it
when we focus on another subject.

Best wishes
for success
and happiness.

Peggy Glenn

160

HINTS, TIPS, ETC.

This last chapter is a collection of small tidbits of information or advice that somehow didn't fit anywhere else. One by one I've latched onto this advice or learned these lessons or listened to (or read) many stories from other people who have worked at home-based typing businesses. This first section probably deserves a chapter all its own because it's so important.

PROTECTION

Some of you may know that my husband (yes, that darling I've spoken about all through this book) has spent more than 25 years in law enforcement and the fire service (sometimes simultaneously). He's been extremely helpful in alerting me to dangers in our house and in the way I conducted business. We've even written a book on family fire safety because we felt so strongly about it. I picked his brain for the following tidbits. This is very serious advice straight from my heart and I truly hope you take it to heart.

In the 7 years I've been self-employed at home, and in the 4 years I've been corresponding on a regular basis with other people across the country who are also self-employed at home, I've heard some pretty grim tales of loss, damage, and heartache that COULD HAVE BEEN PREVENTED. Please give some thought to:

THEFT PREVENTION

1. Mark all of your valuables with an engraving tool. Many police departments or insurance agents will loan you an engraver free. Use your social security

number, birthdate, or driver's license number. Then record the serial numbers of all of your office equipment and personal valuables on a slip of paper and store that paper and any receipts or guarantees in a safe-deposit box. As discussed in the section on insurance, if anything is burned or stolen, you'll be able to prove you owned it in the first place.

2. Take photographs of all of your belongings -- personal and business -- and store the photos in the same safe-deposit box. One picture is worth a thousand ashes or fingerprints.

3. Install dead-bolt locks on your doors -- particularly if you have a sign on your home which advertises your business. As we've already discussed, full-size office typewriters and office machines are hot items on the underground resale market (not to mention all your personal valuables). When installing these locks, though, remember that you not only want to keep intruders out, you also want to be able to escape that home yourself if a fire starts. Don't be imprisoned by your own security devices.

4. Be careful about mentioning your marital status if you are single. During that initial telephone call from a potential customer, particularly if you plan to see customers in the evening, make casual mention of your father, a brother, or a husband (even if they live miles away or don't even exist), to dispel the idea that you are alone and vulnerable to unexpected visits or unnecessary rudeness. We've already talked about dealing with the fear of strangers entering your home. The telephone call is one more place where you can screen out potential problems, and where you can make it very plain that you are self-assured and not the kind of person to be pushed around.

One woman wrote to tell me that after what she thought might have turned into a close call with a customer, she bought a few items of men's clothing, and strategically located the shoes and dirty socks in the living room to give the impression of the ever-messy hubby (I don't have one of those, but some of you might.) In reality, her husband had been dead for 3 years and she wasn't dating, but she didn't want to advertise that fact to any customers. She hasn't been bothered since.

If you're so inclined, take a class in self-defense. These are offered -- free in many instances

-- by police departments, women's clubs, community colleges, neighborhood groups.

5.   Join the Neighborhood Watch program in your area. This is a nationwide citizens-involvement crime prevention and education unit. If there isn't one in your area, ask how you can help to start one. Statistics prove (and burglars admit) that Neighborhood Watch works! You may also prove to be an asset to your neighborhood simply by virtue of the fact that you work at home during the day. You will find yourself becoming more alert to what should and shouldn't be occurring on your block. What neighbor will ever lodge a complaint against your business if you've saved their home from a burglar? Right!

FIRE SAFETY

6.   Install a smoke detector in your home in close proximity to your "office." These devices are lifesavers as well as property savers. Consider your loss as well as your customers' losses if your "office" area were to have even a small fire. Know what the detector sounds like, and know how to react when the detector goes off, and make sure that everyone else in your home knows how also.

7.   Purchase a multi-purpose, dry-chemical fire extinguisher and know how to use it. Install the extinguisher in the kitchen, on a route away from the most likely source of fire -- the stove.

8.   Prepare an emergency escape plan for your home or apartment in case of fire. Discuss the plan with everyone in your family and walk through the plan if possible. Having a plan eliminates panic and deaths.

9.   Use extension cords sparingly, particularly in your office. If you must use them, make sure they are rated to carry the electrical load. If in doubt, check with an electrician, or read our book, DON'T GET BURNED!

10.   When storing paper, chemicals, or other flammable supplies, be very certain that you don't store them too close to a heat source. Never spread papers on electric range burners.

11.   Walk outside and look at your house or apartment numbers. Are they large, in a contrasting color

from the house, unobstructed by shrubbery, well-lighted at night? This will make it easier for customers to find you during the day; it'll also make it easier for fire and police vehicles to find you in an emergency, in the dark, from several feet away using only a spotlight or flashlight.

12. Do you know the telephone numbers for your police and fire departments? Is there a sticker on all your telephones that also identifies your own address and your own phone number? What if a friend, relative, houseguest, or client needed to phone for emergency aid from your home. Would they know your address or phone number? Would they know the emergency numbers?

LIFE SAFETY

13. Complete a CPR course, or at least a Red Cross First Aid course. The information that you will learn in one of these classes will come in handy when you least expect it. The 10-15 hours that this will take will be an investment in your life and possibly someone else's that can't be measured until you need to use it.

On the lighter side:

CAR SAFETY

14. Take a course in basic auto maintenance if you own a car. If you're entirely non-mechanical (as I am), at least know how to check the water, air, oil, brake & transmission fluid, etc. In these days of self-service gas stations, high-priced gas and repairs, some preventive maintenance can pay off for you.

Especially in the early stages of your business, you won't have extra money to be putting into your car. So baby it, pamper it, and take good care of it so it will behave until you can give it more high-class attention. This is particularly critical if you will be offering pick-up and delivery in your business.

Carry flares or portable safety cones in your car, especially if you travel at night, so that you can protect yourself or someone else in case of an accident or mechanical breakdown. Know how to set them out correctly, and be extremely careful when you get out of your car to do so.

HOME / APARTMENT MAINTENANCE

15. Take the same kind of course in basic home repairs/maintenance. If such classes are not offered through your community college or adult education department (or if you live some distance from any place to learn this), check into what your library offers. If you find a book that is easy to read, send away for your own copy or order it at your favorite bookstore. The librarian or bookstore owner can help you find out where to send and how much to send if it isn't in stock.

Consider being prepared for something as simple as knowing how to replace a fuse or fix the circuit breaker: Picture yourself facing a deadline in 30 minutes and you blow a fuse or the circuit trips. What customer is going to understand that kind of excuse no matter how true it is? But if you have fixed it, then take the time to tell them about it and impress them with how much you know and how self-sufficient you are. "I met your deadline in spite of this ... that ... or something else!"

MORE EXTRAS YOU CAN OFFER

* Notary Public: A notary public is an official who is authorized to act as a witness for people who sign legal documents. While the fees for this extra service are modest, it doesn't cost you much of anything to be able to offer it.

Each state sets its own rules, regulations, fees, and requirements for becoming a notary. Basically, you must be over 21, a U.S. citizen, a permanent resident of the area in which you will offer notary services, and have no felony convictions.

Write to the Secretary of State in your state's capitol and request an application and copy of the rules and instructions.

* Checkbook Balancing: Five years ago, I would have hired you if you lived in my area. Many people with small businesses are willing to do most of their bookkeeping chores, but they simply hate balancing their bank statements each month. If you can offer this service to your regular customers, you'll be a rare jewel.

* Photocopying: This will involve a financial
investment for a lease or purchase of a copier, but in
some areas could be a big drawing point for your business.

* Translating: If you live in an area with a high
degree of need for bilingual skills, look around for
opportunities to use them. There are hundreds. This
could range from translating advertisements into a
foreign language, to writing or translating medical
questionnaires for doctors' offices or hosiptals.
There is a professional association of translators.
Write to them for more information if you are interested. Their address is:

        American Translators Association
        P. O. Box 489
        Madison Square Station
        New York, NY 10010

TIMING

    I have a few suggestions regarding when to start
your business. The time of year, the weather, the
trends, and certain scheduling factors can have a bearing on how easily you can implement the processes to
get started.

    These issues are not critical, but if you have a
choice, or if you're able to plan in advance, you can
improve your chances for success by at least considering the following:

    * Academic: It may be wise to start your business
at the beginning of a semester or quarter. If you do
your advertising from early in the term, your name will
be re-occurring in customers' minds. If you are new at
typing academic work, this slow start will allow you to
become familiar with the styles and formats under ideal
conditions rather than under deadline or "rush" conditions.

    The one thing you should be prepared for, however,
is that students frequently wait until the last minute.
The younger students are notorious for this.

    * Business/Commercial: I feel it's best to start
this kind of home-based typing service during good
weather. If your area is subject to snow, lots of

166

rain, tornadoes, hurricanes, etc., you'll want to have your customers "wrapped around your finger" by the time this weather arrives. If you have proven yourself to be reliable and conscientious and downright G-O-O-D under ideal conditions, they will be even more grateful for your services in the poor weather.

Imagine, for instance, how delighted an insurance agent would be to have you help out with claims after a storm after you've given superior service during the summer. If you handle the situation right, you could end up with a sizable paycheck based on "rush" or "hardship" or "emergency" duties. Refer again to my sample bill in the "Customers" chapter. The items I listed were for aggravation, but you can also list items such as: "2 hours in traffic due to blizzard conditions," or "evening/weekend surcharge for rush claims processing."

Be ethical, and be honest, but don't sell yourself short. You are now a valuable business asset. Charge for such dedication accordingly.

* Medical & Legal: These two home-based typing markets may provide business for you on a year-round basis, because people get sick without regard to the calendar, and the courts operate all year long as well. However, in terms of starting your own business and building it up to a level that pleases you, it may be to your advantage to start during a period of good weather.

Your advertising may involve a lot of personal contact, and you want to look your best. This is not always easy at the height of the rainy season or in 30-below + wind-chill = 50-below weather. In Houston or Ft. Lauderdale, looking fresh and professional may not be possible in the middle of the summer when the humidity index is over 90%, either.

As I said, some places in the country enjoy good weather most of the time, so timing may not be a critical factor in a successful start-up. But at least consider your weather, your terrain, your customers, and your way of life when getting ready to make the big step to self-employment.

Careful thought will make the difference between un-employment, self-employment, and (dread, dread) re-employment in a "real job."

TWO LOOKS AT REALITY

You do need to face the possibility of slow times
or disillusionment. What'll you do if you're having
trouble making ends meet? What do you do if you find
yourself with a sudden bill and not enough cash to pay
for it?

Don't panic!!!!!!!!

Don't get discouraged and start looking for a job!

Don't think that it's all over and you can't make
a go of it!

Contact a temporary agency. I did it, and it
wasn't really awful. Remember that month-long vacation
I told you I took one summer? Well, I over-spent my
budget just a little. My MasterCard bill looked as if
someone had gone berserk.

When I returned from vacation, there was no work
waiting for me. So, I had a friend who was a partner
in a new temporary agency. She needed reliable people
to fill clients' orders, and I needed about 2 weeks'
worth of work. We worked out an agreeable rate for my
skills, she found me a job, and I worked at one firm
for the whole two weeks.

The first day was painful because I wore pantyhose
and a skirt to make a good impression. But after I
proved how good I was, I spent the rest of the time in
presentable -- but comfortable -- clothes. At the end
of the two weeks, I said, "Thanks for the opportunity
to work here, it's been fun and I learned some new
tricks, I have all the money I need, don't call me,
I'll call you."

I haven't gone back since. But it was there when
I needed it, and the money came in handy. Besides
that, it was a definite ego-booster to know I was still
so marketable in the "real world." By going through a
temporary agency, I was spared all the formalities,
drudgery, and psychic trauma of filling out job applications, going for interviews, etc. It was bearable, and
it paid the bills. And no guilt at the end of the 2
weeks!

Lastly, if you give it an honest try, if you do
everything "right" and it either doesn't work out or
you don't like it, don't consider yourself a failure.

The only failure is failing to try. There is no such thing as defeat if you at least make an attempt. There is growth in being able to say, "It's not for me."

PROFESSIONAL GROUPS TO HELP

INDEPENDENT PROFESSIONAL TYPISTS NETWORK
(IPTN)

In 1980 I founded the Independent Professional Typists Network (IPTN). Over the years, the organization has grown to nearly a thousand members in nearly all 50 states and some foreign countries. In 1983, the group assumed formal status after being my dream and baby for 3 years.

As stated in the organization's bylaws, the IPTN's purpose is to: "(a) unite owners of independent typing and word processing businesses; (b) provide support to members through education and communication."

To accomplish this, the organization publishes a newsletter, convenes for an annual convention, encourages local chapter formation, and participates in local and regional workshops and seminars. To quote further, "IPTN members are encouraged to participate in a networking process to enhance professional knowledge and personal growth. IPTN serves as a forum and gives members the opportunity to share experiences and insights."

MEMBERSHIP

IPTN is open to all people who do own or are prospective owners of professional typing and/or word processing businesses. IPTN is member-governed and is

administered by elected and appointed officers. The
administrative director and membership office is
located at:

                INDEPENDENT PROFESSIONAL TYPISTS NETWORK
                          12 CHICORY WAY
                         IRVINE CA 92715

     To obtain membership information, please send a
self-addressed business-sized envelope bearing 2
stamps.

                  PRO-TO-TYPE, THE NEWSLETTER

     The newsletter contains such items as: places to
buy supplies at reduced rates, interesting customers,
unusual ways to advertise, out-of-the-ordinary typing
jobs, etc. Some recent newsletter articles topics have
been: an in-depth look at how to arrange for sub-contract help; typing for genealogists; husband and wife
typing or business teams; and a report on the ads that
lure home workers with headlines such as, "You, too,
can make money at home addressing envelopes," or "Home-
makers--hundreds weekly possible!"

     Another issue contained a thorough report by an
accountant on ways to make the bookkeeping part easy.
We've also had a detailed report on how to choose a
word processor for home business use. Each issue contains a book report, news from network members, and
news I've gathered. Some issues have reviews of new
products or new discount supply houses.

     If you have some good information to contribute to
the newsletter, type it up and send it in care of the
administrative office noted above. She'll forward it
to me or to the current newsletter editor. For
instance...

     ...I talked with an Ohio woman last week who took
a vacation to Florida over the Easter break. She had
some typing work to finish, but didn't want to spoil
her trip, so she took the typewriter along in the trunk
of her car. Each morning she got up early, typed for a
few hours in the motel room, and was on her way. That
is one great way to combine work and fun. Her trip was
pleasant, she met her deadlines, and she told me, "I
never could have done this in my other job!" Let's
give her a hand for using her head for something other
than a shoulder ornament.

MEMBERSHIP ROSTER

All IPTN members' names appear on a current list -- state by state -- which is updated regularly. Once you are a member, you will receive the most current roster and you are free to contact another IPTN member in your area or anywhere in the country if you are still skeptical or unsure about your business decision, or if you need a sympathetic ear to listen to your ideas and business plans.

PROJECT OUTREACH

You may have questions after you've finished reading this book. No matter how hard I've tried to be thorough, there may be something unique about your situation that will need a little more explanation. I used to be able to answer personal letters. However, as the volume of mail increased to over 100 letters a week, that became impossible. One of the most exciting features of IPTN is members' willingness to share their expertise and answer questions. Once you become a member of IPTN, someone will be able to help you through PROJECT OUTREACH. "Outreach" questions are handled by referral or in a regular newsletter column.

*   *   *   *

PROFESSIONAL ASSOCIATION OF SECRETARIAL SERVICES (P.A.S.S.)

Of the same caliber, but founded and operated primarily for owners of office-based secretarial services, this professional organization is also one you should consider. I haven't been as intimately involved in its formation or workings, but I have nothing but respect and admiration for the way it is run and the people who are in it. P.A.S.S. was also one woman's dream and it is now a very credible and creditable national organization. For membership information, send a manila envelope with three stamps to:

P.A.S.S.
c/o Secre-Help
2200 E 104th Ave #103
Northglenn   CO 80233

Please tell 'em Peggy Glenn sent you.

*   *   *   *

Here are a couple more, also founded by people who
had dreams, saw needs, and worked harder as volunteers
than they ever had for pay. In both instances, please
mention where you learned about them, and please
enclose a self-addressed, business-sized envelope bearing two stamps. Your thoughtfulness and professional
courtesy will be greatly appreciated.

**NATIONAL ALLIANCE OF HOME-BASED BUSINESSWOMEN
(N.A.H.B.)**
P.O. Box 95
Norwood   NJ 07648

*   *   *   *

NATIONAL ASSOCIATION FOR THE COTTAGE INDUSTRY
P.O. Box 14460
Chicago   IL 60614

POSTAL ZIP CODE LIST

The following are U.S. Postal Service-approved abbreviations for all 50 states and some territories.

The 2-letter abbreviation should always be used on envelopes. The Postal Service requests that the city name not be abbreviated and that the address be typed in all capital letters. For example:

RIGHT: 924 MAIN STREET
HUNTINGTON BEACH CA 92648

WRONG: 924 Main Street
Hunt. Bch., Cal. 92648

Alabama	AL	Montana	MT
Alaska	AK	Nebraska	NE
Arizona	AZ	Nevada	NV
Arkansas	AR	New Hampshire	NH
California	CA	New Jersey	NJ
Colorado	CO	New Mexico	NM
Connecticut	CT	New York	NY
Delaware	DE	North Carolina	NC
District of Columbia	DC	North Dakota	ND
Florida	FL	Ohio	OH
Georgia	GA	Oklahoma	OK
Guam	GU	Oregon	OR
Hawaii	HI	Pennsylvania	PA
Idaho	ID	Puerto Rico	PR
Illinois	IL	Rhode Island	RI
Indiana	IN	South Carolina	SC
Iowa	IA	South Dakota	SD
Kansas	KS	Tennessee	TN
Kentucky	KY	Texas	TX
Louisiana	LA	Utah	UT
Maine	ME	Vermont	VT
Maryland	MD	Virginia	VA
Massachusetts	MA	Virgin Islands	VI
Michigan	MI	Washington	WA
Minnesota	MN	West Virginia	WV
Mississippi	MS	Wisconsin	WI
Missouri	MO	Wyoming	WY

In addition, the Postal Service requests that when a street address is not given or is unnecessary, that the city-state-zip code sequence be all on one line.

173

TELEPHONE MESSAGE SLIP SAMPLE

This is the message-taking slip I designed for my family. I discovered that when I told them what to say and how to say it, I had much better luck with messages. My customers appreciated the thorough way my family takes messages. The impression they created for me was sometimes the first one a customer had of me. In my case as well as in yours, if the message-taker is thorough, courteous, and business-like, it gives my business a great deal of credibility.

I put a stack of these slips by each phone in the house, not just the phone on my desk. I have yet to miss an important call since I started using these little slips. Feel free to copy them exactly or make modifications to suit your family's style and anything else you would like to know.

```
┌────────────────────────────────────────────────┐
│            TYPING CUSTOMER MESSAGE              │
│                                                 │
│                                                 │
│  NAME: _____ │
│                                                 │
│  PHONE #: _____ │
│                                                 │
│  MESSAGE: _____ │
│                                                 │
│  CAN I CALL THEM BACK?_____ │
│                                                 │
│  WHAT TIME?_____ │
│                                                 │
│  ANYTHING ELSE?_____ │
│                                                 │
│  _____ │
│                                                 │
│  _____ │
│                                                 │
│  _____ │
│                                                 │
│  WHO TOOK THE MESSAGE?_____ │
│                                                 │
│  DAY _____ TIME _____     │
│                                                 │
└────────────────────────────────────────────────┘
```

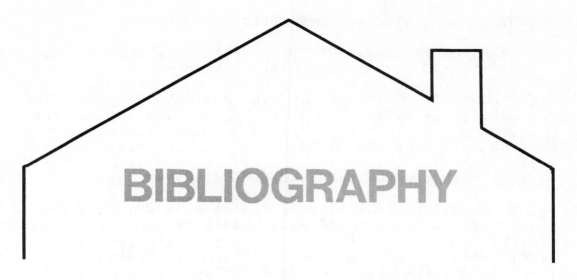

BIBLIOGRAPHY

Below is a comprehensive bibliography of books, magazines, and pamphlets which should provide the answers to any of your business questions. Most of these have already been mentioned in the text of this book, but there are a few new ones, so look closely.

AMERICAN BUSINESS WOMEN'S ASSOCIATION (See page 46)

APA PUBLICATION MANUAL, Publication Sales, American Psychological Association, 1200 Seventeenth, NW, Washington, D. C. 20036.

BEST OF BOTH WORLDS (The), Joan Wester Anderson, Betterway Publications, Inc.

BETTER LETTERS, Jan Venolia, Ten Speed Press.

BLACK'S LAW DICTIONARY, Scribner's, New York.

BUSINESS WRITER'S HANDBOOK (The), Charles T. Brusaw, Gerald J. Alred, & Walter E. Oliu, St. Martin's Press.

COMPLETE GUIDE TO EDITORIAL FREELANCING, C.O'Neill and A. Ruder.

COMPLETE RESUME GUIDE (The), Marian Faux, Monarch Press.

COMPLETE WRITING GUIDE (The), Carolyn Mullins. Prentice-Hall.

CONSUMER INFORMATION CENTER, Pueblo, CO 81009.

THE CRAFT OF FICTION, THE CRAFT OF NON-FICTION, Knott,
    William C., Reston Publishing Co.

DEAR PUBLISHER, Carol Shrum, P.O. Box 726, Clayton CA
    94517 ($4.95)

DENNISON ZIP CODE DIRECTORY.

DOME SIMPLIFIED BOOKKEEPING RECORD #612.

DON'T GET BURNED! A FAMILY FIRE-SAFETY GUIDE, Gary &
    Peggy Glenn, Aames-Allen Publishing.

DON'T USE A RESUME: USE A QUALIFICATIONS BRIEF,
    Richard Lathrop, Ten Speed Press.

DORLAND'S ILLUSTRATED MEDICAL DICTIONARY, W. B.
    Saunders.

EARNING MONEY WITHOUT A JOB, Jay Conrad Levinson, Holt,
    Rinehart & Winston.

EFFECTIVE SELLING THROUGH PSYCHOLOGY, Victor Buzzota,
    Wiley-Interscience.

ELEMENTS OF STYLE (The), William Strunk, Jr., & E. B.
    White, The Macmillan Company.

ENTREPRENEURIAL WOMAN (The), Sandra Winston, Newsweek
    Books/Bantam.

EXERCISE AND WEIGHT CONTROL, Pamphlet #121H, Consumer
    Information Center, Pueblo, CO 81009 (60¢).

FAMILY GUIDE TO CRIME PREVENTION, Manuel Estrella,Jr.
    and Martin Forst, Beaufort Books.

FAMILY WORD FINDER; WRITE BETTER, SPEAK BETTER,
    Reader's Digest Books, Pleasantville, NY 10570.

555 WAYS TO EARN EXTRA MONEY, Jay Conrad Levinson,
    Holt, Rinehard & Winston.

FORM AND STYLE, William G. Campbell & Stephen V.
    Ballou, Houghton Mifflin Company.

HARBRACE COLLEGE HANDBOOK, John C. Hodges & Mary E.
    Whitten, Harcourt Brace Jovanovich, Inc.

HOME-BASED BUSINESSES, Beverly Feldman, Till Press.

HOW TO ADVERTISE AND PROMOTE YOUR SMALL BUSINESS, G. M.
    Siegel, John Wiley & Sons.

HOW TO GET HAPPILY PUBLISHED, Judith Applebaum.

HOW TO PROSPER IN YOUR OWN BUSINESS, Brian R. Smith,
    Stephen Greene Press.

HOW TO PROTECT YOURSELF FROM CRIME, Ira A. Lipman, Avon
    Books.

HOW TO START, RUN, AND STAY IN BUSINESS, Gregory and
    Patricia Kishel, John Wiley & Sons.

IDEAL GENERAL BUSINESS BOOKKEEPING AND TAX RECORD

LEGAL SECRETARYSHIP, Norma Blackburn, Prentice-Hall.

LITERARY MARKETPLACE, Published by R. R. Bowker Co.,
    available in all libraries.

LITTLE ENGLISH HANDBOOK (The): Choices and
    Conventions, Edward Corbett, John Wiley & Sons.

MANUAL FOR WRITERS OF TERM PAPERS, THESES, AND
    DISSERTATIONS (A), Kate L. Turabian, University of
    Chicago Press.

MEDICAL WORD BOOK (The), Sheila Sloane, W. B. Saunders.

MINDING MY OWN BUSINESS, Marjorie McVicar and Julia
    Craig, Richard Marek Publishers, Inc.

MLA HANDBOOK, Modern Language Association, New York,
    NY.

NEW ENTREPRENEURS (The), Terri and Nona Dawe Tepper,
    Universe Books.

PERSONAL COMPUTER BOOK (The), Peter McWilliams,
    Prelude/Ballantine.

PUBLICITY HANDBOOK, Sperry Hutchinson Company.

PUBLICITY: HOW TO GET IT, Richard O'Brien, Harper &
    Row.

REFERENCE MANUAL FOR STENOGRAPHERS & TYPISTS, Gavin
    Sabin, Gregg/McGraw-Hill.

RESUMES: THE NITTY GRITTY, Joyce Lain Kennedy, Sun
      Features, Inc.

ROGET'S THESAURUS, Norman Lewis (Editor), G. P.
      Putnam's Sons, New York, NY.

SMALL IS BEAUTIFUL, E. F. Schumacher, Harper & Row.

SMALL-TIME OPERATOR (How to Start Your Own Small
      Business, Keep Your Books, Pay Your Taxes, & Stay
      Out of Trouble!), Bernard Kamaroff, CPA, Bell
      Springs Publishing.

SPEAK EASY, Sandy Livner, Summit Books.

STANDARD HANDBOOK FOR SECRETARIES, Lois Hutchinson,
      McGraw-Hill Book Company.

SUPPORT SERVICES ALLIANCE, INC. (see page 46)

SURGICAL WORD BOOK (The), Claudia Tessier, W. B.
      Saunders.

TABER'S CYCLOPEDIC MEDICAL DICTIONARY, Clayton L.
      Thomas, M.D., M.P.H. (Editor), F. A. Davis Co.

TWO-BOSS BUSINESS (The), Elyse and Mike Sommer.

UNDERSTANDING MEDICAL TERMINOLOGY, Sister Agnes Clare
      Frenay, The Catholic Hospital Association, St.
      Louis, MO 63104.

WEBSTER'S COLLEGIATE DICTIONARY, available in book
      stores, colleges, and universities.

WEBSTER'S SECRETARIAL HANDBOOK

WHAT IS ECONOMICS, Jim Eggert, William Kaufmann, Inc.

WOMEN WORKING HOME, Marion Behr and Wendy Lazar, WWH
      Press.

WONDERFUL WRITING MACHINE (The), Bruce Bliven, Random
      House, New York, NY.

WORD PROCESSING BOOK (The), Peter McWilliams,
      Prelude/Ballantine.

WORD PROCESSORS AND INFORMATION PROCESSING, Dan
      Poynter, Para Publishing.

WORDS OFTEN MISSPELLED AND MISPRONOUNCED, Ruth Gleeson
        Gallagher and James Colvin.

WORKING MOTHER MAGAZINE.

WORKING WOMAN MAGAZINE.

WRITE RIGHT! Jan Venolia, Periwinkle Press/Ten Speed
        Press.

WRITER'S HANDBOOK, The Writer.

WRITER'S MARKET, Writer's Digest Books.

        I know there are at least 300-400 more excellent
books out there that will help you with any aspect of
your business. This list represents only those books
I've read myself or which have been highly recommended
by my closest business colleagues. Check your local
library for copies, check your favorite neighborhood
bookstore, check in the large chain bookstores. If you
have any trouble locating one of these books, ask the
public librarian or bookstore clerk to help you look it
up in Books in Print, the book that lists all books in
print. If the book you want is no longer "in print"
write directly to the publisher for more information.

        Good reading, best of luck with your business. I
hope you've enjoyed this book as much as I've enjoyed
writing it for you. Type it with pride!

INDEX

Dear Reader,

Use the form below to order additional copies of this book, a copy of <u>WORD PROCESSING PROFITS AT HOME</u>, a copy of <u>DON'T GET BURNED!</u> <u>A Family Fire-Safety Guide</u> that I wrote with my husband, a copy of <u>KEROSENE HEATERS:</u> <u>A Consumer's Review</u> (and safety manual), or a cassette tape on which I am interviewed about my experiences in setting up and running my home-based typing business.

Although it's not exactly best-seller material, I hope you give more than a passing thought to fire safety. Remember, that if you lose your home to fire, you're also out of work. I'll admit I never gave it a thought, either, until I married a fireman. Then I heard on a weekly basis the tragic stories of folks who didn't think or weren't prepared. I am offering a discount on this book because I truly want you to have a copy and read it. It could save your life -- and your livelihood.

TO: AAMES-ALLEN PUBLISHING CO
        1106 MAIN STREET
        HUNTINGTON BEACH   CA 92648-2719

FROM: _____
        Name

        _____
        Address

        _____
        City/State/Zip

Please send me the following:

____   WORD PROCESSING PROFITS AT HOME $14.95
____   HOW TO START & RUN...TYPING BUSINESS   14.95
____   DON'T GET BURNED (regularly $7.95)   5.00
____   KEROSENE HEATERS   3.75
____   Cassette Tape   7.95

        TOTAL FOR MERCHANDISE   _____

        Plus 6% tax for Californians   _____
        Plus $1 shipping each item   _____

        TOTAL ENCLOSED (check or money order) _____

484